FIVE MILLION STEPS ON A JOURNEY OF HOPE: THRU-HIKING THE APPALACHIAN TRAIL

BOB GRAU
(BUCKEYE FLASH)

First published by Dog Ear Publishing
4010 W. 86th Street, Ste H
Indianapolis, IN 46268
www.dogearpublishing.net

ISBN: 978-1-4575-1809-6

This book is printed on acid-free paper.

Printed in the United States of America

TABLE OF CONTENTS

10/10/18

Neal,

Thru-hiking the AT far exceeded my expectations as to scenic beauty, adventure, and challenges.

I hope my story inspires you to undertake a new adventure in your life. Perhaps, you may want to TAKE A HIKE!

God bless,

Bob Shaw
(Buckeye Flash)

MY AT AWAKENING

October 2, 2009, is a day that I will always remember as it is emblazed in my mind, for that is the day that I decided to thru-hike the Appalachian National Scenic Trail, commonly called the Appalachian Trail or simply the AT. It is the nation's most well-known footpath and stretches over 14 states from Georgia to Maine.

Most people who attempt to thru-hike the AT get the desire many years or even decades before they actually attempt to do it. Often as a child, teenager, or young adult, they read a book about the AT. It captures their imagination about what it would be like to hike from Georgia to Maine within one year. It certainly would be a worthy goal, a life-changing experience, and an adventure of fun and excitement.

What made me different from other thru-hikers was that, amazingly, I had never hiked previously. I loved sports, and to me hiking was not a sport. I thought of hiking as merely a walking exercise for those who had little interest in sports. Certainly there were more fun things to do such as swim, ski, and play golf, tennis, or softball.

I was retired in October 2009, and I knew virtually nothing about the AT. However, when I saw Part One of the program called "Appalachian Impressions" on public television, I was hooked. I immediately knew that I was going to attempt to thru-hike the AT. The AT grabbed me and wouldn't let go. I felt like a man possessed. How could that have happened?

The television program told the story of AT thru-hikers in 2004. It depicted beautiful scenery and vistas, and it offered the opportunity to experience nature in all of its elements. I would see places and things that I had never seen and would be impossible to see in any other way. It presented the many challenges that thru-hikers face, including rain and cold weather, steep and rugged terrain, months of arduous effort, and being away from family and friends for an extended time.

At the end of the first hour of "Appalachian Impressions," I was distressed as I realized that the show was only Part One. It ended at the half-way point of the trail. When would I be able to see the rest of the story? I was thrilled to discover that Part Two would air a week later. Yet, even before seeing Part Two,

I knew that I would attempt to become a thru-hiker! That thought truly amazed me as a non-hiker. I was thoroughly smitten with the upcoming adventure and challenge of a lifetime.

Could I succeed in this challenging endeavor? My experience with the outdoors consisted of merely several canoeing trips of a week or less with friends. On those trips at the end of the day, we unloaded the canoe and set up camp for the night. We had fun canoeing in many places including the Au Sable River in Michigan, St. Croix in Wisconsin, Buffalo River in Arkansas, Green River in Kentucky, and the boundary waters on the Minnesota/Canada border.

FACTS ABOUT THE AT

I spent countless hours researching a variety of hiking topics. I began taking notes, and soon I had filled a large file folder. Two great sources of relevant information were from the Websites of the Appalachian Trail Conservancy (ATC) and the Appalachian Trail Long Distance Hikers Association (ALDHA), where I printed the online version of the *Appalachian Trail Thru-Hiker's Companion*. It served as my guide book while I was hiking the trail.

I learned many facts and a great deal of interesting information about the AT. It transverses six national parks, such as the Great Smoky Mountains National Park and Shenandoah National Park, eight national forests, and numerous state parks and forests. A thru-hiker must navigate over terrain that varies widely. At times the trail is a moderately level dirt path. At other times, it may consist of pine needles through a forest, wooden boards or logs crossing wetlands, a pile of rocks, tree roots, slippery mud, chest-high underbrush, creek beds, and vertical-rock scrambles. On most days thru-hikers make steep ascents and descents of thousands of feet over a rugged mountain trail.

The AT changes in length each year due to constant rerouting of various sections in order to prevent erosion, accommodate land acquisitions, and maintain sections of the trail needing repair. The length of the AT in 2009 was 2,178.3 miles before increasing to 2.179.1 miles in 2010. Its length in 2011 was 2,181.0 miles when I thru-hiked it. If only I had hiked the trail in 2010, I could have shaved nearly two miles off my trek.

The Appalachian Mountains, which are the most rugged in the eastern United States, are among the oldest in the world. In 1921 Benton MacKaye wrote a journal article about the use of the skyline of the Appalachian Mountains. By 1930 Myron Avery took some of MacKaye's ideas along with his own and got support for the AT. In 1937 the AT was opened as a wilderness trail along the eastern seaboard, running from Georgia to Maine. Then in 1948 Earl Shafer became the first thru-hiker of the AT. Three years later in 1951 Gene Espy became the second thru-hiker.

Several million people hike some part of the AT each year. Most are day hikers, who return home at the end of their outing. Every year many hikers attempt to thru-hike the entire AT. Most of these hikers start at Springer Mountain, Georgia, which serves as the southern terminus. It is about seventy miles north of Atlanta and is the starting point in the spring for northbound hikers. These hikers are trying to thru-hike to Mt. Katahdin, the northern terminus in Baxter State Park in Maine. Every year some south-bound thru-hikers start in Maine in late spring or early summer heading toward Georgia. Most hope to finish at Springer Mountain by Thanksgiving or Christmas.

A thru-hiker climbs over 471,000 feet or more than 89 miles going over 270 mountains. That distance is equivalent to climbing Mt. Everest about 16 times. Climbing an average of 216 feet/mile on the 2,181-mile trail, a thru-hiker takes about five-million steps to complete the journey.

The AT is managed by the National Park Service and the non-profit Appalachian Trail Conservancy (ATC). There are 31 trail clubs, which are responsible for most of the daily work needed to keep the trail open. Each club monitors a section of trail and builds and repairs shelters and other structures. Volunteers contribute hundreds of thousands of hours to the AT every year.

Upon learning of my hiking plan, many people asked me if I had read *A Walk in the Woods* by Bill Bryson. Soon I had the funny book and read it in a few days. I searched for other books written about the AT and found some excellent ones. Each offered a different twist, new facts or experiences of thru-hikers.

WHAT WERE YOU THINKING?

When I first told my wife, Nancy, about my new passion, she thought I had gone crazy. Why would I want to thru-hike the AT? She knew I wasn't a hiker. Of course she was worried about my welfare. I could get injured. In addition, I would be gone for perhaps six months. She would have to take on the responsibilities that I had, such as balancing the checkbook, maintaining the yard, doing the grocery shopping, etc. When a friend asked Nancy if she would visit me while I was hiking the trail, she immediately said, "He knows where I live." That remark didn't sound like a ringing endorsement to me in my attempt to thru-hike the trail.

Our two daughters, Cindi and Michelle, took another view. They thought that the adventure was "cool" or "awesome." Of course I agreed with our daughters. I imagine that they had doubts that I would make it all the way to Maine. However, they never expressed those thoughts to me.

HIKING EQUIPMENT AND GEAR

Since I had never hiked, I had very little hiking equipment or gear—only a bulky sleeping bag, an inflatable air mattress, and an old headlamp, which I had used on previous canoe trips. Within a few weeks of deciding to thru-hike the AT, I went to a local outfitter. The young man who worked there had done some hiking and was knowledgeable about the gear and equipment in the store. However, he was not a long-distance hiker, and he had not hiked on the AT. He was not well informed about what gear and equipment it takes to thru-hike the AT successfully. He suggested that I purchase a two-person tent weighing nearly five pounds. The tent was nice and roomy, so I bought it. I spent about $1,500 on the tent, backpack, pack cover, down-filled sleeping bag rated at 30 degrees, small stove, butane-fuel canister, hiking boots, wool socks, water filter, and some packages of dehydrated food.

The items that I wish that I hadn't bought were the tent, backpack, pack cover, and water filter. The salesman never mentioned any concern I should have about the weight of the pack or amount of space the items would take. During the subsequent months before beginning the hike, I spent about $200 on clothing to wear while hiking. In my naivety, I believed my gear and equipment needs had been met, and I was ready to go. How wrong I was! I would end up buying many of the same items twice.

PHYSICAL PREPARATION

Physical exercise has always been a big part of my life. I have been on a regular exercise routine for decades. I have lifted weights and run numerous road races from five miles to marathons, so the rigor of daily hiking was something that I was pretty sure I could handle. However, there is really no way to simulate or train for the physical difficulties and fatigue faced by hiking at least eight hours nearly every day for up to six months.

In early 2010, a friend of mine, Bill Beuther, mentioned that he was eager to go to the White Mountains in New Hampshire to hike. He had first hiked there as a boy with his father and had returned numerous times to hike the majority of its mountains. I knew that the White Mountains were considered the most difficult area on the AT, so I suggested that we make the trip together. In August 2010, we spent three days hiking there.

On our first day of hiking, we climbed Mt. Lincoln (5,089 ft.). On our second day, we climbed Mt. Lafayette (5,260 ft.). On our third day, we attempted to climb Mt. Washington (6,288 ft.), but we experienced rain and cold weather about half-way up. We turned around and descended. By the time we had reached the bottom, the weather had improved greatly, so we decided to hike Mt. Cannon, a ski mountain. After reaching the summit of Mt. Cannon (4,100 ft.), we took the cable car down.

Hiking in the White Mountains showed me how difficult the AT would be and helped me develop the confidence that I could handle the steep and rugged terrain. However, the trails we took in the White Mountains were not those I hiked on the AT. In fact I did not actually hike on the AT at all during the trip. My thru-hike of the AT was completely a new adventure.

In fall 2010 I began to hike short distances twice a week in the area near my home. Many times I hiked in the Cuyahoga Valley National Park with two retired colleagues, Verna Vanderkooi and Mark Higgins. We often hiked about five miles on relatively easy trails. At times I carried a backpack weighing as much as thirty pounds, while at other times I did not carry a backpack. On some occasions, snow and ice covered the ground.

RAISING MONEY FOR CHARITIES

After I decided to thru-hike the AT, I felt very selfish. I had made a decision to leave my family and friends for perhaps six months. Although I expected to experience a great deal of excitement and adventure from the hike, no one else would get any benefit from it. What could I do to reduce this negative feeling? How could I involve my family and friends on the nearly 2,200-mile journey?

Then the thought hit me of how others could benefit from or be involved with my hike. I could get charitable sponsors to support my effort. I decided to seek a penny for each mile that I hiked to benefit charity, but what charity should I chose? I recalled that, after my retirement, two former colleagues had gotten me involved in the recreational outdoors. I took several canoe trips with Harvey Kassebaum and Jeff Holzworth. Both of them had suffered from devastating illnesses. Harvey fought lymphoma for years and was deceased, while Jeff was in a hospice facility with Alzheimer's disease. Then I thought of my brother, Jim, who died in July 2007 from melanoma, so I selected three charities to benefit from my hike: the Leukemia/Lymphoma Society, the Alzheimer's Association, and the Society for Melanoma Research.

I hoped to secure 100 charitable sponsors to donate a penny for every mile that I hiked. I could raise $2,181 with just 100 patrons. To get the word out, I created a five-page handout about the AT and my upcoming hike, asking directly for charitable support. I gave the handout to family, friends, former colleagues, neighbors, and acquaintances. I distributed the handout to some people personally, while others got it by e-mail or through the U.S. Postal Service.

After I secured 100 sponsors, I wanted more. When I exceeded 200, I set a new goal of 300. Finally, after securing over 300 patrons, I ran out of time. Only a few people that I contacted rejected my request. I appreciated that my cousin, Patty Mattson, obtained over 30 people who pledged financial support. I was excited that many benefactors pledged more than a penny per mile. I calculated that if I were successful and completed the entire length of the AT, I could raise about $7,500.

I promised to send the charitable sponsors a photo and a weekly update on my progress. Once I was hiking, I called my daughter, Cindi, and read to her a brief description of my most recent AT experience. She wrote on paper what I had said and then typed it on a blog (http://grauathiker.blogspot.com). She attached a photo that I had texted to her of something interesting that I had seen on the trail. Cindi did a fantastic job! I got great feedback about the blog. Many people reported that they felt as if they had hiked the trail vicariously with me. At the end of the hike, there were about 25,000 hits on the blog.

Once I was on the AT, I used the thought of hiking for the three charities as a motivator, especially when the trail became difficult or times were tough. For each mile that I hiked, I was raising well over $3 for the charities. I also met a few other thru-hikers that were raising money for charities they had chosen.

HIKING ALONE

Sixty percent of thru-hikers begin their hike alone, as I did. It is difficult to find someone who is willing and able to thru-hike the AT. That is not surprising as most people are sane, have jobs, and have a life outside of hiking. Only one friend, Jim Hill, expressed a desire to thru-hike the trail with me. However, he owned his own business and was still several years from retirement. He could not leave his business for such a long time. Everyone else wished me well on my journey, but no one expressed an interest in joining me. I fully expected that it would take some time to find a hiking companion. I would need to meet a person with a temperament and personality that I enjoyed, who matched up well with me in hiking pace and speed, and who shared similar daily mileage goals. In that case, I would enjoy hiking with a partner.

TRAIL NAMES

On the AT, most hikers select their own trail name or are given one by another hiker. The trail name creates a new identity from what a person has back home. In addition, it is much easier to remember a hiker's trail name than his or her real name. Trail names typically are one or two words that describe something about the hiker. Some are humorous like Bear Bait or Swamp Dawg.

I thought about what trail name I would want. I chose "Buckeye Flash." Although some people think of a buckeye as a worthless nut, it is often identified with Ohio. Many people know that the athletic teams at The Ohio State University are known as "Buckeyes." I chose flash as part of my trail name because it referred to my tendency to walk fast and to my college days at Kent State University, known as the "Golden Flashes."

MEETING THRU-HIKERS

In September 2010, I received a call from a friend and former colleague, Dick Stagliano. He was at Acadia National Park in Maine. He had met a young man, Mike Kaufman, who just days before had finished thru-hiking the AT. Dick got Mike's phone number for me. Mike lived only about five miles from me, and I looked forward to talking with him.

A few weeks later, I called Mike and arranged to meet him for lunch. He described his experience on the trail including what equipment he liked and the places he had stayed. I peppered him with many questions. I even arranged a second meeting several weeks before my hike began. While Mike was hiking on the AT, several hikers asked him what his trail name was. He answered repeatedly, "So far I don't have a trail name." As a result, Mike was dubbed "So Far."

In fall 2010, I read in the newspaper that another thru-hiker, Jeff Alt, was scheduled to speak at a local bookstore. I was excited to hear about his AT adventure. His presentation was informative and funny. It included photos he had taken on the AT during his thru-hike in 1998. Jeff had raised more than $16,000 during his hike for Sunshine Inc. of Northwest Ohio, where his brother, Aaron, is a resident. The non-profit organization aids the developmentally disabled and mentally retarded. After Jeff's presentation, I bought a copy of his book, *A Walk for Sunshine*. Proceeds from the sale went to the non-profit organization.

While I was waiting to meet Jeff after his presentation, I began to talk with a man, Mark Remaklus, who was sitting near me in the audience. I quickly learned that he had also finished thru-hiking the AT just a short time before. Mark's trail name was "Severance." He grew up and lived in Lorain County near Cleveland. When he got laid off in 2010, he decided to thru-hike the trail. How lucky was I? I went to the bookstore to hear Jeff talk about his interesting AT experience. Then, in addition, I met yet another successful thru-hiker.

Mark told me how the trail had been such a positive experience for him that he wanted to thru-hike it again! Why would he want to do that? Unfortunately for me, Mark soon moved to accept a job. However, we communicated by e-mail and talked on the phone several times as well. Mark's advice to me about many aspects of hiking the trail was extremely valuable.

I truly appreciated all the information and great advice I received from the three thru-hikers I met before my hike began. All of them were such positive people and a joy to know. Each spoke of his hike as a life-changing experience and reflected on the memories he had. Not all of their experiences were positive, but their joys far outweighed the difficulties. While I was hiking the AT, I thought of them often and what they had told me. In a similar fashion, I hope to meet future thru-hikers and share my experience. My wish is that I can help others as much as Mike, Jeff, and Mark helped me.

THE LONG WAIT

In October 2009, I decided to hike the AT, but the earliest I could start was in 2011. The long delay was due to three pleasure trips that I had already booked, as well as other commitments I had made for spring/summer 2010. I initially planned to begin the hike on April 1, 2011—no April Fool's Day joke. I thought that most of the winter weather would be about over by then. However, as I gave more thought to when I should begin, I decided to start on March 22, 2011. That way, in case of injury or illness on my part or a family emergency at home, I could take a few weeks off and still have time to finish at Mount Katahdin in Baxter State Park in Maine before October 15, the last day of the year that the Park is open. Furthermore, in September and October, it's possible that Park Rangers there can shut down the trail due to inclement weather. Hiking the trail when it is closed can result in a felony.

GOOD FORTUNE FROM A COOKIE

The month before my hike, I ate lunch at two Chinese Restaurants. At the first restaurant, China Buffet, my fortune cookie stated, "Don't judge the height of a mountain until you have reached the top." I thought of that statement many times on the trail, as there were many mountains that have a false summit. It looked as though I had reached the top of the mountain, only to have the trail level off and then begin to ascend again. At the second restaurant, Mandarin House, my fortune cookie stated, "A new voyage will fill your life with untold memories." I would certainly agree that the AT thru-hike created memories that I will always cherish. When I reflect on the predictions of both fortune cookies, I still get a chill up my spine.

HOSTELS

I wanted to take advantage of staying at hostels on the trail, so I spent many days researching them on the internet. I made note of how close the hostels were to the trail, what services they provided, and what they charged. Although hostels vary widely regarding the services and amenities offered to hikers, most are a good value. Some hostels are modern and very clean, while others are old and rustic. Most have indoor plumbing, while a few have an outdoor privy and solar shower. Although the majority charges a fixed fee, often between $15-$30/person per night, some are free with a donation gladly accepted. Typically the larger the fee, the more services offered. Most hostels have laundry facilities for hikers to use, but some actually wash and dry the hikers' clothes. Many also provide a shuttle service to various destinations for a fee, while some will transport hikers to/from the trail and to a grocery store and restaurant for free. A meal, linens and towel, internet access, and air-conditioning are offered by some as well, and most will accept or mail packages for hikers. Many of the owners have hiked the AT and will go out of their way to be helpful.

GETTING TO THE TRAIL

On Monday morning, March 21, 2011, I flew from Cleveland Hopkins Airport to the Atlanta Hartsfield Airport. On the plane I wore hiking boots and clothes that I planned to wear the following day to begin my hike. Several days before my flight, I shipped some of my gear to the Hiker Hostel in Dahlonega, Georgia. I planned to stay there the night before beginning my hike. The box that I shipped contained my stove, pan, cup, water filter, tent, headlamp, air mattress, and sleeping bag. After arriving at the airport, I went to the luggage area and claimed my backpack. It had some of the things I would carry on the hike, including clothing, crocs, food, toiletries, and miscellaneous items.

I made my way to the MARTA station and boarded the train to North Springs, the most northern rapid transit station. After exiting the train, I met a man who dreamed of thru-hiking the trail. Kevin Pflederer (trail name "Kebban") was waiting to be picked up and shuttled also to the Hiker Hostel. He was from Indianapolis, Indiana, and had recently retired as a firefighter. He had previously hiked sections of the trail, but this would be his first attempt to thru-hike the AT.

After waiting 20 minutes, we were picked up by Leigh Saint. She and her husband, Josh, own and operate the Hiker Hostel. It is not far from Springer Mountain, the southern terminus of the AT. Leigh drove us to Amicalola Falls. Many thru-hikers stay there at a lodge and some then hike eight miles on an approach trail to the start on Springer Mountain. Kebban and I were then joined by three women, whom Leigh had arranged to meet there. All of us boarded Leigh's van and were on our way to the hostel.

In the van, I told Leigh that Jason and Agata Ketterick, the son and daughter-in-law of a friend and former colleague, Mike Ketterick, were in the area. They were conducting a Leave No Trace (LNT) training program. Shortly before we reached the hostel, Leigh said to me, "Look at the car ahead of us. It is a LNT vehicle." What a coincidence! I recognized Jason and called him on my cell phone. He was amazed that I was in the car immediately behind him. He and Agata decided to drive to the hostel and have a short visit with me and to meet Leigh and Josh.

The Hiker Hostel is a large modern structure, which can accommodate many hikers. It was nearly full of eager hikers that evening. I picked Kebban's brain for advice on every hiking topic I could think of. He emphasized, "Hike your own hike. Don't let others decide for you what to do."

Many hikers gathered in the basement of the hostel that night for dinner, and everyone prepared his or her own meal. I overheard a hiker say that he was nervous and scared. He wondered if he would make it and questioned whether he had the ability and, more importantly, the "right stuff" to reach Mt. Katahdin. Was he prepared physically and mentally to reach his goal?

I was not worried or afraid before my hike. I felt as physically prepared as possible, and I was determined to succeed, yet I did feel uncertain about what was ahead. A major concern was that an injury could derail my journey. That possibility was made clear to me by a local man (Charlie Martin) who had attempted to thru-hike the AT in 2003. He was in outstanding physical condition at the start of the hike. However, a knee injury in New England resulted in surgery and ended his dream. Every aspiring thru-hiker is just one step away from possible serious injury. I fully expected to sustain an injury at some point in the nearly 2,200-mile hike over steep and rough terrain. It seemed inevitable.

Before I left home, I decided to use a backpack on the trail given to me by a friend, Ralph Caddell. Although I had bought a backpack at a local outfitter, it was difficult to find what I was looking for in the deep pack. It had only two small side pockets. The backpack which Ralph had given me had several side pockets, some with zippers. I could locate things far easier than in the store-bought backpack.

I gathered all my equipment and the gear that I had shipped ahead, as well as what I had taken as luggage on the plane. I spread all of it out on my lower bunk, and it covered the bed completely. After I filled the side pockets and every nook and cranny of the external-framed backpack, I could barely get the pack closed. I realized that I had too much stuff, yet it seemed like everything in the pack was a necessary and much desired item.

THE HIKE BEGINS IN GEORGIA

Day 1—Tuesday, March 22, 2011

The morning was sunny and beautiful, as hikers were blessed with an unseasonably warm day for March. I enjoyed a large and delicious breakfast prepared for the hikers. Then I went outside to get a breath of fresh air. I noticed a hanging scale on the hostel's covered porch. I hoisted my ready-to-go backpack up on the scale with much difficulty. When I saw that my pack weighed 53 pounds, I was amazed and shocked. Could that be correct? I thought that it must be a mistake.

Two other hikers soon came out on the porch and weighed their packs. One pack weighed over thirty pounds, and the other was slightly over forty pounds. The two hikers concluded that the scale was correct. I lifted each of the other packs. Unfortunately, both seemed to be considerably lighter than mine. I did not show my dismay, but I knew then that I was in for a more difficult journey than I had previously anticipated. I simply said, "It is what it is!" In reality, I was rather embarrassed.

In hindsight, I should have loaded my backpack at home with all my gear and weighed it. I had planned to do that, but there always seemed to be more pressing things with which to be concerned. Another reason for not weighing it was that I was either adding or removing things to take on the hike up to the time I flew to Atlanta, so I put it off and never did weigh it. Common sense somehow had avoided me. Then I had a perplexing thought. What would I have removed at home to reduce the weight of my pack if I had known that the loaded pack weighed 53 pounds? I had no idea, as everything in the backpack was there for a reason.

A few minutes later, I was in Josh's van with seven other hikers. He drove us several miles to the Big Stamp Gap parking lot at U.S. Forest Service Road 42 and dropped us off. From there we began a one-mile hike going south on the AT toward Springer Mountain. That one-mile hike could be considered a warm up since it didn't count as a mile hiked on the trail. We were simply getting to the starting point of the 2,181-mile AT.

I reached the top of Springer Mountain (3,782 ft.) at about 10:00. It was a surreal experience. Was I merely dreaming this? As I signed the register, I felt a sense of anxiety and excitement. I took a photo of Kebban, and he took one of me. I noticed the bronze plaque embedded in a rock that displayed a hiker. It stated, "Appalachian Trail. Georgia to Maine. A footpath for those who seek fellowship with the wilderness." I hoped that my fellowship with the wilderness would be a positive one!

Moments later I began the long-awaited hike of roughly five million steps by following the first white blaze heading north toward Maine. The rectangular white blazes are two-by-six inches and usually painted on trees. Sometimes they appear on rocks, posts, signs, or other structures. There are about 160,000 white blazes marking the trail—80,000 in each direction. A pyramid-shaped pile of rocks called a cairn marks the trail above tree line. Blue blazes indicate side trails that lead off the AT to a shelter, water source, and privy (outhouse). They can also lead to a point of interest, such as a great vista or historical landmark. Any hiking done on a blue-blazed trail does not bring a hiker any closer to the final destination of Mt. Katahdin in Maine.

Kebban stayed at the top of Springer Mountain and took more photos than I did. We were not hiking together, but I expected to see him later that day at the Hawk Mountain Shelter. We planned to stay there on the first night of the hike. About 250 shelters dot the trail. Many are right on the trail or a short distance down a blue-blaze side trail. Some are farther from the trail. Most shelters are three-sided structures with a lean-to roof and open front. Usually a water source and a privy are reasonably close. Most shelters have a picnic table and fire pit. Camping is usually available in the same area. The shelters tend to fill up early in the spring, especially if it is raining, or foul weather is threatening. Mice can be a problem. Some hikers experience mice running over their bodies and even getting into their packs. Snoring can be a concern too, as hikers sleep side-by-side on the floor of the shelter.

I had read enough about the trail to realize that hiking long distances in the early going was a mistake. It takes time to develop "hiking legs." Over time I planned to increase the miles that I hiked. As I headed north, I settled into a comfortable pace. As I walked along, I sipped water from my Camelbak, a water bladder which was nestled in my backpack. I was pleased that I didn't have to take off my pack to get a water bottle as many hikers did. After hiking for a while, I took my first break. It felt great to take a short rest and enjoy a snack. I marveled at the fine weather I was experiencing in March on the first day of the hike.

After hiking nearly eight miles, I saw a sign indicating that the Hawk Mountain Shelter (3,200 ft.) was .2 of a mile down a blue-blaze path. As I reached the shelter about 4:00, I felt relieved. I had survived day one of the steep and rugged mountains in Georgia! However, I had created hot spots on both heels, and several of my toes were sore. I looked for a good spot to set up my roomy, two-person tent.

I happened to find a camping spot next to a thru-hiker named "One Step." I thought that his trail name was a good one, as I reflected on the saying, "Take one step at a time to reach your goal!" After a thru-hiker takes about five million steps, he should be very near or at the summit of Mt. Katahdin! One Step laughed when I said, "I am Buckeye Flash now. However, if I don't make it to Mt. Katahdin on this hike, I'll be known as Buckeye Flash in the Pan."

One Step related how seven years earlier his dream of thru-hiking the AT had vanished. He suffered a stress fracture, and every step he took caused him pain. After he left the trail, mental torment merely replaced the physical pain. After hearing One Step's story, I thought of the anguish I would experience if I were unable to fulfill my dream of thru-hiking the AT.

I went down a blue-blazed trail about 300 yards to get water. Kebban and another hiker were standing at a small stream, but they were not filtering their water. Instead, they were adding a chemical called Aqua Mira to their water bottles. I asked how it worked. Kebban explained, "Aqua Mira kills bacteria in the water, but it does not change the taste." It seemed to be an easier way to secure drinking water than filtering it as I was doing. In addition, not carrying the water filter would save weight and create valuable pack space. After just a day on the trail, I realized how important that was.

After I filtered my water, I went to the shelter to "cook" my meal. To say that I cooked a meal is really a stretch. All I did was merely boil water in my titanium pan and pour it into a pouch of store-bought dehydrated food, such as spaghetti, lasagna, or beef stroganoff. I stirred the contents so that the hot water would begin to rehydrate it. Then I had to wait several minutes for it to cool slightly. Voila—supper was ready. It certainly didn't taste as good as real home-cookin', but it was edible. An advantage of eating out of the food pouch was that there were no dishes to wash.

After finishing dinner, it was almost time to go to sleep, but first I needed to secure my food so that black bears would not steal it. Bear cables or bear boxes were often available at the shelters, especially where bears had been a problem in the past. They were relatively easy to use, and it took just a minute to secure the bag out of reach of any bear. I used them whenever they were available.

I had bought an Ursack bag to protect my food from bears and rodents where bear cables or bear boxes weren't available. The Ursack bag is made of flexible, light-weight, "bullet-proof" fabric, which is the same material from which police vests are made. A strong, thick plastic bag with a pressure-seal fits inside the outer bag. If the inner bag is properly sealed, the food contents are supposedly odorless. If the outer bag is properly knotted, bears or rodents can't get inside.

I did not see anyone else on the trail that had a similar bag. Where there were neither cables nor boxes available, I did not have to take several minutes to find a tall tree to hoist my bag over. I could merely place my Ursack bag away from my tent tied to a tree or simply laid on the ground. I never had a problem with any kind of animal getting into my food.

Day 2—Wednesday, March 23, 2011

It was a cooler day than the first with the temperature in the 50-degree range. I was one of the last hikers to leave camp as I began hiking about 9:00. Within a few minutes, I saw more rhododendrons than I have ever seen in my life. Although the rhododendrons were not yet in bloom, there were plenty of small white and yellow flowers along the trail.

It didn't take long to realize that the 53-pound pack was a real problem. I concluded that it was not a weight that I could carry for more than a few days. I found comfort in knowing that if I could just get to the outfitter at Neels Gap, I could greatly reduce the weight of my pack. I could buy a lighter backpack and smaller tent, and I would also eliminate non-essentials. Then I would stand a good chance of successfully thru-hiking the AT. But first I had to suffer! As I was climbing a mountain or simply walking the trail on a relatively flat area, I looked for a rock or log where I could stop and rest my pack for a few minutes without removing it. The pack began to cut into my lower back. I folded my jacket and placed it between my lower back and backpack. The jacket worked pretty well as a cushion, reducing the discomfort! Relief!

Carrying a 53-pound pack

The terrain seemed a little steeper on day two, and I descended over 500 feet before climbing Sassafras Mountain (3,300 ft.). Then I descended another 500 feet before climbing Justus Mountain (3,224 ft.). After hiking more than seven hours, I reached my destination of Gooch Gap Shelter. Although I had hiked only slightly more than seven miles, I was completely satisfied.

Day 3—Thursday, March 24, 2011

The highlight of the day was experiencing trail magic for the first time. Trail magic occurs when unexpected acts of kindness or hospitality are done for thru-hikers. Getting a gift from someone a thru-hiker does not know and will probably never meet generates a feeling of gratitude. It uplifts the hiker's body and spirit. Trail magic is provided most often by thru-hikers who have experienced it themselves while hiking. They realized how wonderful it was to be treated so kindly and want to return the generosity shown them. Trail magic is almost always found on the AT near a road access and is usually accompanied by a note stating who left the gift. A thru-hiker is often asked to sign his name in a spiral notebook of the provider. The thru-hiker usually writes a brief thank-you note too in the notebook.

At noon, there were several cans of soda resting above a trail sign at Woody Gap (GA 60). Although I was not exceptionally thirsty, I was thankful to the stranger that had left them. As I rested at Woody's Gap sipping a soda, I began to realize that the next day I should reach Neels Gap. There was an outfitter and hostel there and also cabins to rent. I had been told that the cabins were quite nice and reasonably priced at $60/night. I read in the *Appalachian Trail Thru-Hiker's Companion* that a cabin could accommodate four hikers and had a kitchen with refrigerator and stove, television, sofa, bathroom, beds, linens and towels, and an attached porch. To top it off, the owner provided free laundry service. Wow! That description sure sounded better than the nearby hostel, where for $15/night, I would need to sleep on a bunk with a roomful of snoring hikers. It seemed that all I had to do was to find three other hikers with whom to share a cabin. I didn't think that would be difficult, as there were a lot of north-bound hikers on the trail heading toward Neels Gap.

During the day, I climbed Big Cedar Mountain (3,737 ft.). From there I made several ascents and descents until I reached Slaughter Creek Campsite (3,800 ft.) at 5:30. Although I felt really tired from the long day, I had hiked 12.5 mile. The temperature had dropped considerably, and my fingers struggled to function properly as I set up my tent.

I walked downhill to the water source. Filtering water from the stream was a real effort. My body temperature was declining rapidly since I was standing still. I returned to my tent and set up my stove to boil water for a hot meal. As I finished dinner, it was getting dark. I quickly surveyed the area and found the base of a small tree not far away where I could tie my food bag. Then I snuggled into my sleeping bag to get warm and enjoyed a restful night's sleep.

Day 4—Friday, March 25, 2011

As I woke up in the morning, there was frost on the outside of my tent. My water bottle had a thin layer of ice in it. As I took down my tent and packed my backpack, I hurried as much as possible. I started to hike at a slightly faster pace than normal in order to generate body heat. My effort produced only moderate success. I had hiked nearly 28 miles over the first three days, and I was only about three miles from the outfitter at Neels Gap and the Blood Mountain Cabins, but first, I would need to climb Blood Mountain (4,458 ft.), the highest point in Georgia on the trail. Some say that Blood Mountain was named due to Indian wars in the seventeenth century between the Creek and Cherokee. Battles there and at Slaughter Gap were said to have turned the mountain red with blood. Another theory is that the red-colored lichen and Catawba rhododendron were the reason for the name.

By mid-morning I reached the Blood Mountain Shelter. I took a break and talked for several minutes with some section hikers. They looked askance at the size and weight of my external-frame backpack. I sensed that that they thought I would never make it to Maine. I told them that I was planning to reduce weight and buy a new backpack and a smaller and lighter-weight tent at the outfitter at Neels Gap.

Section hikers typically hike part of the trail for one or two weeks each year. Some try to hike the entire length of the AT over a period of years. If a section hiker completed 200 miles each year, it would take about 11 years to finish. Section hikers have the advantage of knowing they will be going home in a specific time, such as in a week or two. The downside of section hiking is that, just as the hiker's body begins to adjust to the rigors of hiking longer distances, the hike is over until the following year. Then the process of developing "hiking legs" must begin again.

The trail descends over 1,300 feet from Blood Mountain to Neels Gap (3,125 ft.). After I began what should have been a hike of less than three miles, I had difficulty locating the trail. The white blazes seemed to disappear. I struggled on the steep and slippery rock terrain and fell for the first time. A few minutes later, I fell again, and one of my hiking sticks bent in half.

The second fall, which was so close to the first, really upset me. I took the broken hiking stick and flung it as far as I could. I was in a remote area well off the trail, and the stick landed in dense underbrush. I thought of the "Leave No Trace" philosophy, which I supported. On a positive note, I imagined that no human being would ever see my broken hiking stick again. I expected that it would rust out before anyone would stumble across it so far off the trail.

I wandered for about twenty minutes in the wilderness, using my remaining hiking stick for support. My pack seemed to take on added weight. Finally, I had to admit to myself that I was in a bad way. I had a sinking feeling in my stomach. So close to Mountain Crossings, but yet so far. What should I do? I decided to head in the general direction that I thought I had come. I said a prayer for divine help as I headed back up the mountain trudging through the underbrush. I had very little idea where the trail was, and my progress back up the mountain seemed painfully slow. Eventually, I got near the top and spotted a white blaze. A sense of relief came over me, and I praised the Lord for getting me back on the trail. I felt as if I had been lost, and now I was found. The misadventure took the better part of an hour.

I was struck by the fact that the AT is truly a wilderness trail when I reached Neels Gap at U.S. 19 & 129. It was only the second paved road I had seen since I had started hiking four days before. My spirits and outlook were lifted as I knew that my life was about to change for the better! The trail led directly across the road to a full-service outfitter called Mountain Crossings at Walasi-Yi Center. The store and attached hostel are ideally situated about 31 miles from Springer Mountain. I can't imagine a better location for an outfitter. Nearly all of aspiring northbound thru-hikers make it to Mountain Crossings. However, it is estimated that 20% of those hikers quit the trail there. The remaining hikers are ready-made customers. They need to resupply, and many of them want to buy new equipment. I fell into both of those categories.

As I talked with a few hikers at Mountain Crossings, I learned that I had missed trail magic by less than an hour. As a service project, a group of Boys Scouts had provided a free lunch for hikers. If I had been able to stay on the trail as I descended Blood Mountain, my stomach would have been full. I was hungry and purchased a sandwich from a stocky man. I certainly would not have guessed that he was an accomplished thru-hiker. I heard him called "Baltimore Jack." I recognized his name as his reputation had preceded him. He had thru-hiked the trail eight times and had the reputation of a fun-loving rascal.

Once I had finished eating, I inquired where the Blood Mountain cabins were. I was directed about a quarter mile down the highway. Upon reaching the cabins, I met by a hiker I knew. He directed me to the "Squirrel Cabin," where I was able to stay with two hikers I knew well—Kebban and One Step. Another hiker staying at the cabin was "Double Check," whom I had not met previously. After checking out the room where I would sleep, I took my laundry to the office. A woman greeted me and said it would be ready within a few hours.

Then I went back to my room, picked up my backpack, and returned to the outfitter at Mountain Crossings. I met with the store owner, Winton Porter. I told him of my dilemma—my 53-pound pack. He had probably dealt with a situation like mine hundreds of times. I am sure he thought of me as what I really was—an inexperienced and naïve hiker. After I had laid out all of the contents of my pack on a picnic table, the shakedown began. Winton told me what gear I didn't need—too many pants, shirts, and towels, for example. He also suggested I add long underwear for some expected cold nights, especially in the Great Smoky Mountains National Park.

Winton didn't need to convince me that I needed a new tent and backpack or to send home my water filter. I replaced my two-person tent, which weighed nearly five pounds. I bought a Big Agnes Copper Spur tent that weighed less than half as much. I replaced the external-frame pack weighing nearly five pounds with a two-pound ULA pack. I got rid of the bulky water filter and added two small bottles of Aqua Mira that most thru-hikers use. That decision reduced my pack weight by about a pound and freed-up valuable space. I bought new hiking sticks, light-weight long underwear, a rain jacket, and water-proof gloves. I really appreciated Winton's help. He thanked me for my business, which amounted to well over $1,000.

I was excited to return to the cabin with all of my new items. It was just like show-and-tell in elementary school, as I displayed my new equipment to my roommates. Then I went to the office and got my neatly-folded, clean clothes. I was amazed at such service. When I was back at the cabin, I laid out everything I had on my bed. It seemed to take forever to decide where in the pack I should put each item. I realized that there was a lot more to hiking the trail than just the physical aspect.

The hikers began discussing when they first had the desire to thru-hike the AT. All of them related that they had wanted to hike the AT since they were a child or teenager. On the other hand, my dream of thru-hiking the AT had occurred when I was age 65. I joined the "club" at an advanced age.

Day 5—Saturday, March 26, 2011

I was the last hiker to leave the cabin in the morning. It was the first time that it rained on the hike. Although I was not eager to hike in the rain, I thought of the saying I had heard, "No rain, no Maine!" Rainfall is essential to provide a source of water for hikers. I walked back to Mountain Crossings and sent my unneeded and excess gear home. I also took some items I thought that I may need later on the trail and "bounced" the box to a hostel, where I planned to stay several weeks later. If I did not need to open the box then, I could bounce it ahead again to another location at no additional cost.

I put my old hiking stick and the external-frame backpack into the "hiker box" at the hostel for anyone to claim free of charge. Hiker boxes are located at every hostel and at some shelters. They contain excess food, discarded clothing, and unwanted miscellaneous items of hikers. I figured that someone would eventually claim both my backpack and hiking stick. The pack that I had been carrying was in good shape, but it was too big and heavy for me. When I hoisted my new backpack with my gear including food and water onto the scale at Mountain Crossings, I was delighted that it weighed 35 pounds. I knew I could handle that weight.

I went outside to resume the hike, but the rain had picked up, so I retreated into the store. I inquired about rain pants, but the store did not have any in my size. Finally, the rain appeared to let up, and I was ready and eager to resume my hike with my lighter-weight pack! I exited the store and stood under an overhang, surveying the dark sky that indicated a long period of rain.

A south-bound hiker arrived. He told me that he had camped off the trail a few miles north of Neels Gap the night before. A black bear had taken his food bag that was hung in a tree. I was about to head in the direction the bear had been. A few weeks later, I was told that the bear had continued to create havoc for campers. As a result, the trail was closed for many miles north of Neels Gap, and the rogue bear was being hunted.

I finally headed north on the AT about noon. I was thrilled by the lighter weight of my pack.

Carrying the new lighter backpack

It was certainly not light, but it was manageable. I could hike at a slightly faster pace with it, but more importantly, I would not need to stop to rest nearly as often. I felt like a new man with increased confidence. I sensed that I had a good chance of successfully completing the thru-hike. Even the thought of a bear on the trail wanting my food caused only slight concern.

The chilly rain continued intermittently nearly all day. Less than an hour after leaving Neels Gap, my hands were completely wet and cold. The waterproof gloves I bought did not even seem to be water resistant. Winton Porter had told me that he was not sure how waterproof the gloves were as they were a new item. The rain did not dampen my spirits on the dismal day. In fact, the cool day seemed to give me added energy. I was out to prove something to myself and maybe to others as well. I wasn't a slow hiker, who needed to rest once or twice a mile. As I crossed paths with several hikers heading south towards Neels Gap, their typical greeting was, "Hi, how are you?" My response was, "I'm just great. I couldn't be better." Well, that did stretch the truth just a tad! A little less rain would have made for a less muddy trail and dryer feet!

In the afternoon, I greeted a group of Boy Scouts and their troop leader heading south. About 7:00, I reached my destination of Low Gap Shelter (3,050 ft.). I was pleased that I had hiked almost 11 miles on the dreary day. The elevation changes for the day had been relatively moderate with ascents and descents each totaling roughly 2,000 feet.

I was eager to stay in a shelter for the first time, but it was full. I looked for a spot to set up my tent, but there were no good locations. Reluctantly, I set up my tent in the least muddy area I could find. I was cold and wet, and I did not want to cook. However, I decided I should to warm my body. I ate a dehydrated meal of pasta primavera. I fell asleep about 8:30.

Day 6—Sunday, March 27, 2011

I awoke at 7:30 a.m. and was amazed that I had slept 11 hours. It was the longest night's sleep I got on the entire hike! The last time I had slept so long I was in college. The rain had stopped in the morning. Mud was everywhere—on my shoes, clothes, tent, and backpack. It was not fun putting on my damp, dirty clothes and packing my wet, muddy gear into my backpack.

I walked to the shelter to eat my breakfast. There were two teen-aged brothers still there. They were from Delaware and were home-schooled. Ben was 13, and Tom was 17. The boys' parents thought the hike would provide an excellent learning experience for them. Their older brother had hiked the trail some years before.

I noticed a black plastic bag on the ground next to the shelter. I asked the boys if the bag belonged to them. They said it contained trash left by the Boy Scouts who had recently stayed at the shelter. I surmised that the group I had passed the day before might be the culprits. Whoever left the bag violated the "Leave No Trace" philosophy—if you carry something in, carry it out. Leave the area as much as possible as if you had never been there.

I resumed my hike heading toward Unicoi Gap. For many hours the visibility was minimal as a cloudy mist covered the mountains. Then, as if someone opened the shades at home, the clouds lifted, and the sun came out. It was a difficult day of hiking with rocks and boulders of all sizes littering the trail—a preview of what it would be like later hiking in Pennsylvania. The trail that day wore on me physically and mentally, and I appreciated my hiking sticks for keeping me upright.

I stopped in the mid-afternoon to take a break and call my wife. I told her that I was alone, sitting on top of Blue Mountain (4,025 ft.) in Georgia. All I could see in every direction were mountains. It felt so good to share the peaceful moment with a loved one.

It was nearly a 1,200-foot descent to Unicoi Gap. By the late afternoon I completed hiking more than nine miles and just over 50 miles total. I crossed the road at GA 75 (Unicoi Gap) and walked into a parking lot. There was a car at the other end. A woman got out and began to walk toward me. I thought about asking her if she would give me a ride into Helen, Georgia. Before I could speak, she said, "Would you like a ride into Helen?" "Would I ever!" was my response.

The woman's trail name was Red Hat, and she was a trail angel. Her home was in Texas, but she was spending the spring as a trail angel in Georgia and North Carolina, offering free rides to hikers. She had hiked the trail in sections over the last several years. Red Hat drove me about nine miles into Helen, which is Georgia's Gatlinburg. Many buildings in Helen look like chalets. I was eager to stay at the Super 8 Motel that offered a hiker rate of $35, including a continental breakfast. At the motel, I washed my muddy tent and Tyvek ground cover in the shower. Then I set up my tent in the room to dry.

Day 7—Monday, March 28, 2011

In the early morning, it was raining lightly as I headed to the laundromat. Having clean clothes and a dry tent made me feel revitalized. The weather forecast was for rain to end later in the day. Four hikers, who had stayed at the Blood Mountain Cabins a few nights before, were taking a zero day, a day of no hiking. They simply wanted to enjoy Helen and relax. The rain stopped by mid-morning, and the skies brightened. I walked to Betty's Country Store and Deli to resupply. Then I began to hitch a ride back to Unicoi Gap.

I wondered how many cars it would take before I got a ride. On the 22nd vehicle, not counting commercial vehicles or a police car, I was picked up. The driver was a retired man (Daryl) who had operated a liquor store in the area for 20 years. I asked him if he had ever been robbed at the store. Although he hadn't, he did have two dangerous situations. A regular customer who was drunk had pulled a gun on him. Daryl reasoned with the man to put the gun away, and there was no further problem. Then he told a second tale of refusing to sell to another regular customer who was stoned. That man chased him around the store carrying a straight razor. Daryl was not harmed in either occasion. He did not make a police report either time because he didn't want to lose either man's business. Daryl was another trail angel. He drove eight miles out of his way to get me back to the trail.

I began hiking from Unicoi Gap (2,949 ft.) about noon. Since it did not rain the rest of the day, I was pleased with my decision to hike. I had a long climb of nearly 1,100 feet up Rocky Mountain (4,017 ft.) before descending to Indian Grave Gap (3,113 ft.) Next, there was a long climb up Tray Mountain (4,430 ft.) before descending to Addis Gap (3,304 ft.).

Most hikers suffer foot problems at times on the trail. Long descents are especially murderous on a hiker's feet, and blisters are common. I had three sore toes and a hot spot on both heels. I stopped hiking and treated the problem by cutting strips of moleskin. I wrapped a strip around each injured toenail and along the back of each heel. It didn't solve all the problems, but it helped!

I climbed up Kelly Knob (4,276 ft.) before I began the final descent to Deep Gap Shelter (3,550 ft.). I thought that I was the last hiker to arrive at the shelter at 7:20. I was pleased that I had hiked over 13 miles in about seven hours. The shelter slept 12 hikers and was full. I was not surprised to see Kebban in it. We talked briefly and shared our desire to stay at the Blueberry Patch Hostel the next day. I quickly set up camp using my headlamp to see where to put the tent stakes. It was a cold night, and the temperature dropped into the thirties.

Day 8—Tuesday, March 29, 2011—Week 2

Although I only needed to hike less than four miles to reach Dicks Creek Gap, I was on the trail soon after sunrise. I wanted to be sure of getting the shuttle there to the Blueberry Patch Hostel because it had bunks for just seven hikers. I knew that a free shuttle would arrive about 9:30.

When I reached Dicks Creek Gap (2,675 ft.), I was surprised to find the young brothers, Ben and Tom. They had reached the shelter the prior evening about midnight. Since they did not want to set up their tent in the dark, they slept on the ground under the shelter, even though there were just a few feet of clearance. They resumed hiking about 5:00 a.m. The boys were short of money and the Blueberry Patch Hostel was free for thru-hikers, so they wanted to be certain to stay there. Ben and Tom reminded me of Christmas bargain hunters who camp all night in front of a retail store in anticipation of "Black Friday." Kebban and a few other hikers soon appeared. The shuttle pulled in about 9:30 as expected, and several people got out and began to resume their hike. All of us who were waiting were driven to the hostel. Gary Poteat and his wife, Lennie, operate the hostel as a Christian ministry to serve hikers, not to make money. I came away with a real respect for both of them.

At the hostel I was able to claim a lower bunk in the corner of the room. I laid everything in my pack on the bed to sort. Near my bunk was a boot dryer. I had never used one before. I placed my damp boots upside down on the machine. The dryer puts out a low level of heat to dry the boots slowly. Gary collected the hikers' dirty clothes to be washed.

In the early afternoon, Kebban and I were happy to accept a free shuttle into the town of Hiawassee. It was good to be back in the civilized world for a day. We ate at Daniel's Steakhouse, which offered an all-you-can-eat (AYCE) buffet. The food was good and plentiful, and we left the restaurant, moaning with the delight of very full stomachs. We walked to the library to check our e-mail before going to a supermarket to resupply. Gary picked us up at 5:00 and drove us back to the hostel. When we returned, we folded our clean clothes. It was a great day!

That evening at the hostel I talked with a thru-hiker, who had arrived later in the day. His name was George Lowry (trail name Swamp Dawg), and he was happy to share his AT experiences. Although he had section hiked the entire trail over many years, this was his first attempt to thru-hike the AT.

Day 9—Wednesday, March 30, 2011

At breakfast, I sat next to 13 year-old Ben. When the scrambled eggs were passed, he filled his plate. By the time the eggs reached the last hiker, there were none left. One hiker said, "The eggs are gone because Ben took a plateful." It was true! Ben had to be very embarrassed. Gary asked Lennie to scramble a few eggs for the deprived hiker sitting at the end of the table.

As Gary drove the hikers back to Dicks Creek Gap, I thought about hiking with Swamp Dawg. I contemplated the tradeoff of hiking alone versus hiking with a partner. I was hoping that Swamp Dawg's hiking pace would be compatible with mine. I liked hiking alone because I could decide when to start and stop, when and how long of a break to take, and where to camp. However, having a hiking partner offered several advantages. It would ease loneliness and offer the opportunity to share the trail experience. Everyone has heard the statement that misery loves company, but everyone enjoys sharing joy as well. There would be a second set of eyes to spot the white blazes. There would be someone to snap a photo of me. Finally, hiking with a partner would provide protection from possible harm and offer assistance in case of injury or physical problems.

After we reached the trailhead, I put on my backpack. I waited a moment for Swamp Dog. As we began to hike together, I was just a few steps in front of him. We talked about our family, our past jobs, and our lives at home. Swamp Dawg's wife had died of cancer several years before. He described her difficult ordeal of fighting the disease. As we hiked, I felt a real bond begin to develop between us.

NORTH CAROLINA

In the afternoon after we had hiked nine miles, we came to a small wood sign nailed to a tree marking the Georgia/North Carolina border. One state down, 13 states to go! A few hours later we reached our intended destination of the Muskrat Creek Shelter (4,600 ft.). We had hiked nearly 12 miles for the day. It was difficult to find a level spot to camp. I realized eventually that the place I had picked to set up my tent was not very desirable. The slope of the land was slightly downhill, and I kept sliding toward the bottom of the tent. I vowed not to make that mistake again.

As we ate dinner at the shelter, we agreed to begin our hike the next morning at 7:30. I was pleased with our first day of hiking together. It seemed that our hiking pace was similar. I had found a hiking partner, and I hoped that we could hike together all the way to the summit of Mt. Katahdin.

Day 10—Thursday, March 31, 2011

The morning was cold, and there was frost on my tent. I was happy to begin hiking so that I could create some body heat. By mid-morning I had seen several trees that had blown down either on, near, or next to the trail. Some blow downs had occurred years ago, and the dead trees were rotting. Other downed trees had occurred recently, as evidenced by green leaves. It made me realize that I did not want to be hiking or in my tent in a violent thunderstorm near tall trees. I had the disturbing thought that if a large tree hit me, I would likely be killed. From that point on, I always looked at the condition of trees near where I was considering setting up my tent.

The highest elevation of the day was at Standing Indian Mountain (5,498 ft.). We hiked over 12 miles and reached the Carter Gap Shelter (4,540 ft.) about 5:00. At dinner time, I went to the shelter and prepared my meal. Supper time was also a good time to talk with other hikers, write a few sentences about my day in the register, and sign my trail name. Some hikers wrote lengthy reviews about their day and even demonstrated their artistic talents in the register, which was usually just a spiral notebook.

Over the next few weeks, Swamp Dawg served as my mentor. I relied on his judgment and experience. It was encouraging to hear him say that after a month I would be a seasoned hiker. His common-sense advice was refreshing. He stressed that there was no need to make any excuses for stopping and taking a break. He said it was important to not wait until a small problem became a big problem. If I experienced any sort of difficulty while hiking, such as a stone in my shoe or misaligned backpack, I should stop immediately to fix the problem. He suggested that we simply hike at a comfortable pace. He reminded me that the hike was not a race but a journey. Some hikers, especially younger ones, hike too

The AT goes under a "blow down"

fast and complete too many miles in the early going. To emphasize his point he said, "Too fast, too soon, to home!"

Swamp Dawg's guidance reminded me of advice given to me by a former colleague, Jim McGinty, before I ran my first marathon. Jim said, "Begin running at a very slow pace. You will feel like you can and should run faster, but don't do it. Over time, very gradually increase your pace. Your body will accept and respond well to the gradual change. You will pass far more runners in the race than pass you." I followed his recommendation in two marathons that I ran, and it worked just as Jim said.

Day 11—Friday, April 1, 2011

This was the date that I had previously thought of starting to hike the AT. I felt pleased that I had changed my plans to start in late March. I had already hiked over a hundred miles. I was on my third day of hiking with Swamp Dawg, and we were determined to reach Franklin, North Carolina. Swamp Dawg had made a reservation a few weeks previously for a two-night stay (Friday and Saturday) at Haven's Budget Inn. He knew that the annual trail festival was occurring that weekend, and motel rooms would be in short supply. Getting to the motel would not be easy, and it would require hiking nearly 16 miles. That would be more than three miles farther than I had ever hiked.

We got an early start about 7:00. The weather was good, and we kept our breaks short. The toughest part of the day was scaling Albert Mountain or simply "Big Albert" to Swamp Dawg. It involved a nearly 1,000-foot steep climb from Betty Creek Gap (4,300 ft.) to the summit of Albert Mountain (5,250 ft.). Although I climbed tougher mountains later, Big Albert took my breath away.

About 5:00 we reached Winding Stair Gap (3,760 ft.) at U.S. 64. Haven's Budget Inn in Franklin was just ten miles down the road. We began trying to hitch a ride. As the day waned and the sun disappeared, the wind gradually increased. Our chilled bodies were not generating any heat. After a half-hour, we called for a shuttle that cost each of us $10. Five minutes later, an attractive woman in a van stopped and asked if we wanted a ride into Franklin. Unfortunately, we had to reject her free offer and wait another 15 minutes in the cold for the shuttle. Swamp Dawg and I shared the $40 cost of the room at the motel. Sleeping in a bed instead of in my tent was a real treat.

We walked to Elmore's Fish Fry for dinner. Swamp Dawg and I decided to order the medium-sized Perch dinner. It turned out to be plenty of food to eat. After the meal, I approached the manager and said, "I have a complaint. The perch dinner was so good that I overate and am quite uncomfortable." He smiled and replied, "Thank you for your complaint." Swamp Dawg and I agreed that the fish dinner was outstanding.

Day 12—Saturday, April 2, 2011

This was my first zero day. As Swamp Dog and I walked back to the motel after breakfast, we were offered trail magic. A man, who figured we were in town for the AT festival, offered us a ride to a supermarket. The driver did not know Swamp Dawg or me, but he looked vaguely familiar. His trail name was Survivor Dave, and he had endured a serious bout with cancer. He said that he lived in Atlanta and provided a shuttle service for hikers. Then I remembered that I had seen him talking with two hikers at the Big Stamp Gap parking lot exactly twelve days earlier, the morning that I began my hike.

I thought of how the hiking community was indeed a small world. I had never expected to see Survivor Dave again, but here I was riding in his car. As he was driving us from the supermarket back to the motel, he offered to stop first at an outfitter. I was pleased, as I had wanted to buy rain pants ever since I could not find my size at Mountain Crossings. At the outfitter I bought a pair of rain pants that I wore often on the rest of the hike.

Day 13—Sunday, April 3, 2011

In the early morning, I boarded an old school bus at the motel with Swamp Dog and several other hikers. We were driven a short distance to the First Baptist Church for a free pancake breakfast. We shared a table with Ben and Tom. I was reacquainted with Red Hat, my trail angel, who drove me from Unicoi Gap to Helen, Georgia a week earlier. As we were finishing eating, I was flabbergasted when Ben complained that the breakfast was not very good. Although the breakfast was not as delicious as the one at the Blueberry Patch Hostel, it was a free meal.

Shortly after we arrived back at the motel, we boarded a large van to take us back to the AT. We stopped first to pick up hikers staying at another motel. After a ten-minute delay, we were on our way, or so we thought. Our driver was an older southern gentleman who moved very slowly. His protruding stomach got in the way of the steering wheel. Our next stop was to get gas. It took the driver at least 45 seconds to get out of the van and at least another minute to get ready to pump the gas.

I said, "At the rate the driver is moving, we may not get to Winding Stair Gap until nightfall." Then Swamp Dawg said, "Let me remind you of the cultural differences between the South and the North. Time is not a big issue in the South." Then he cracked up everyone in the van with his next comment. He said, "Don't worry! We'll eventually get to the AT after the driver goes to Uncle Jethro's to pet the dog and then stops to see the new tooth of his young niece, Ida." My side hurt, and I couldn't stop laughing.

We finally arrived at Winding Stair Gap (3,760 ft.) after 10:00. The sun was shining, and the temperature was about 60 degrees. During the day, we hiked up the treeless mountain summit of Wayah Bald (5,342 ft.). I climbed the stone observation tower there to take in some breathtaking views. It was built by the Civilian Conservation Corps in 1937. Many hikers were resting against the retaining wall that surrounds the tower area. Some had removed their shoes and socks and were just enjoying the sun. I thought about doing the same, but the effort did not seem to be worth the time or trouble.

We were delighted to experience trail magic near the end of the day. As we arrived at Burningtown Gap (4,236 ft.), many hikers were drinking soda or beer and talking with a man and a woman, who were standing in front of their van. Within a few seconds, I recognized the woman. She had offered Swamp Dawg and me a ride into Franklin a few nights before. Unfortunately, we could not take advantage of her kind offer. After we drank a soda and ate a delicious donut, we hiked another mile to the Cold Spring Shelter (4,920 ft.), arriving about 7:00. We set up camp after completing nearly 16 miles.

NANTAHALA OUTDOOR CENTER

Day 14—Monday, April 4, 2011

We began hiking by 7:30. After completing five miles, we reached the Wesser Bald Observation Tower (4,627 ft.), formerly a fire tower. I climbed the structure to see a panoramic, majestic view. Fontana Lake and the Great Smoky Mountains National Park dominated the landscape to the north.

After a nearly 3,000-foot descent from Wesser Bald, we reached U.S. 19 about 3:00. There the trail passes through the Nantahala Outdoor Center (NOC), an outdoor-adventure center offering whitewater rafting, mountain biking, and horseback riding. Our first stop was at the retail store to buy a cold soda. Between the store and River's End Restaurant, where we later ate dinner, the AT crosses a pedestrian bridge over the Nantahala River.

We stayed at Base Camp, where several buildings are built along a walkway. Each structure has a few separate rooms that are very basic with two bunks. The room cost was $18/person plus tax. A nearby building has a bathroom, laundry facilities, large kitchen, and dining area.

Swamp Dawg and I arrived at our room first and claimed each of the lower bunks. Later two other hikers arrived. One was an older man who wore a heavy knee brace. The other was a middle-aged man with a huge backpack. He said he was carrying about a three-week supply of food. Judging by the size of his pack, I believed him. I could not understand why he was carrying so much food. I immediately thought that neither of the men would be able to complete the hike. After sharing the room with them, I never saw them again.

By early evening, it began to rain heavily and turned colder. The wind picked up and thunder and lightning made for a stormy night. All of us in the room were thankful that we were in an enclosed building. The weather forecast for the next day was not much better, as the rain and cold temperature were expected to continue.

Day 15—Tuesday, April 5, 2011—Week 3

Although it was not raining in the morning, many hikers planned to take a zero day because of the weather forecast. Swamp Dawg and I decided to take the chance of getting wet and began hiking just before 8:30. The risk paid off, as the weather improved throughout the day. We had a 3,300-foot climb up Cheoah Bald (5,062 ft.) and then nearly a 2,000-foot descent to a small picnic area at Stecoah Gap. It was about 5:00, and we had hiked nearly 14 miles. We decided to set up camp a few hundred yards down a closed dirt road behind the picnic area. Swamp Dawg suggested that we walk down the dirt road past a small bend so that we could not be seen from the main road.

We were pleased that the day which first appeared rather dismal turned out to be dry. After we were asleep, a coyote came very near our tents and let out one-long, blood-screaming howl that immediately woke us. It caused the hair on the back of my neck to rise. The coyote had to be within 50 feet of us, but I wasn't about to unzip my tent to greet him. No further howls occurred, and I eventually went back to sleep.

Day 16—Wednesday, April 6, 2011

At breakfast, Swamp Dawg and I laughed as we theorized that the coyote was merely protesting our presence in his territory. At 6:30 p.m., after hiking over 15 miles in eleven hours, we reached the Fontana Dam Shelter (1,810 ft.), known as the "Fontana Hilton." It is the largest shelter on the AT and sleeps 24 hikers on two levels. An indoor bathroom is located about 100 yards away, where I enjoyed taking a hot shower.

Swamp Dawg was pleased with our progress and with a smile on his face commented, "If we keep movin', the law will never catch up with us!" I was too tired to cook. The weather was mild, so I simply ate a bagel with peanut butter and jelly for supper. Before the shelter filled up, we each claimed a spot on the lower level for our sleeping bag and gear. The evening marked the first night that I slept in a shelter on the AT. I heard snoring during the night.

Day 17—Thursday, April 7, 2011

Swamp Dawg suggested that we take a zero day, my second on the trail. We waited nearly an hour on the cool morning for a shuttle to arrive to drive us a few miles up the winding road to the Fontana Village. We resupplied at the Fontana General Store and went to the laundromat.

For lunch, we walked to the Fontana Lodge. After we sat down, One Step came in, and we suggested that he join us. I hadn't seen him for a few weeks. Sadly, it turned out to be the last time that I saw him. Months later I heard that One Step's dream of thru-hiking the AT was dashed again.

We walked back to the general store after lunch to get the shuttle to return to the Fontana Dam Shelter. While we were waiting, a thru-hiker realized that he had received too much food from home. He laid out all the excess items that he did not want to carry and offered it free to any hiker. I picked up a few energy bars and candy bars.

That evening Swamp Dawg decided to stay in the shelter for the second night. I set up my tent about 100 feet from the shelter to avoid hearing snoring. The weather forecast was favorable, and I thought that I would get a better night's sleep in my tent than I had the previous night in the shelter.

THE SMOKIES

Day 18—Friday, April 8, 2011

Swamp Dawg and I left the shelter and walked toward the Fontana Dam about 7:30. We went to a self-registration facility at the visitor's center to obtain a backcountry permit to enter the 72-mile trail through the Great Smoky Mountains National Park (GSMNP). Then we crossed over the Fontana Dam, the sixth highest dam in the U.S at 480 feet. I wasn't looking forward to hiking in the Smokies, as my newly replenished food supply seemed to greatly weigh down my backpack. Swamp Dawg had convinced me that I should carry enough food for five-to-six days to get through the Smokies. However, I would have preferred to carry no more than a four-day supply.

Entering the Smokies with Swamp Dog

A recurring problem that continually must be faced is how much food to carry. The answer depends on how far it is to the next resupply point. All hikers look forward to getting resupplied with a sufficient amount of food to fuel the body and produce enough energy to hike. It's estimated that a thru-hiker will eventually burn 4,000-6,000 calories once an all-day regiment of hiking is attained. The ideal situation is to run out of food just at the point of resupply.

Most hikers would rather error on the side of having too much food rather than running out. However, carrying an excess amount is problematic. The extra weight causes discomfort, fatigue, and reduces the amount of miles that can be hiked. Over-buying is a problem that most hikers experience often when they resupply. A hiker's eyes become too big for his backpack. In a supermarket, every kind of food appeals to a hiker. Each tempting item is shouting out to the hungry hiker, "Buy me! I really taste good!" Of course, I fell for that appealing line at times. After resupplying, the added weight of the backpack is indeed a physical burden. At that point, most hikers wish they had bought less food. However, the good news is that after an hour or two of carrying the heavier pack, a hiker's body seems to adjust somewhat to the load. The pack is still heavy, but it seems to be more manageable.

At the entrance to the GSMNP, we had our picture taken by Bear Bait. He was hiking with Blind-as-a- Bat, a legally blind hiker from Seattle. More than nine million people visit the Smokies annually. It is home to the most diverse forest in North America. There are more than 100 species of trees, 1,570 species of flowering plants, 60 species of mammals, more than 25 different species of salamanders, and 2,000 varieties of mushrooms.

On our first day of hiking in the Smokies, we had ascents of 4,100 feet. Our highest elevation was on a mountain called Devils Tater Patch (4,775 feet). During one ascent, Swamp Dawg gave me the nicest compliment a thru-hiker could ever get. He said, "Buckeye Flash, I think that you are part mountain goat!" That is the equivalent of telling a woman that she looks beautiful!

After hiking about 14 miles, we reached the Russell Field Shelter (4,360 ft.) at 5:45. Regulations in the GSMNP require hikers to stay in a shelter if space is available. Only thru-hikers are permitted to tent camp at shelters. Since the 14-person shelter was full, I was pleased that I could stay in my tent.

After supper, we hoisted our food bags, using the bear cables available. Black bears are not interested in hurting or eating people, but they're interested in the food of humans, if it is available. Nuisance bears have occasionally caused problems in the past. Although as many as 600 black bears live in the Park, I did not see any during my trek in the Smokies. My guess is that one or more bears probably saw me and went in the other direction. Bears are said to be generally more afraid of people than people are of bears.

The GSMNP employs ridge runners to oversee a designated area of the trail. The job involves seeing that regulations are met, maintaining the area around each shelter, checking hikers for permits, and aiding and assisting hikers in need. The ridge runner at the Russell Field Shelter told me that there had not been any bear problems within the Park in the spring. He identified a small flower that is extremely prevalent on the trail as Spring Beauty. It is small with white petals and purple stripes coming down from the center giving it a pink tint.

Although I occasionally saw hikers with dogs on the AT, they are not permitted in the GSMNP or in Baxter State Park in Maine. There are steep fines for violators. A hiker with a dog must arrange to board the pet before entering either park. I would not want the responsibility of caring for a dog while hiking, including feeding it and cleaning up after it. Horseback riding is permitted on about 550 miles of the park's hiking trails. I did not see any horses, but I did see evidence that horses had left. I took great care **not** to step in the evidence!

Day 19—Saturday, April 9, 2011

We began hiking shortly before 7:30 on a beautiful day. In the afternoon, Swamp Dawg stopped to rest numerous times for several minutes. He told me that he was holding me back, and I should go on and hike without him. I flatly rejected that suggestion. I greatly enjoyed hiking with him and considered him a friend. Furthermore, I felt indebted to him for his kind and sage advice. His health, though, was a real concern to me. Our highest elevation for the day was at Thunderhead Mountain (5,527 ft.) We eventually reached the Siler Bald Shelter (5,460 ft.) at 7:00. We had hiked nearly 15 miles. Once again the shelter was full, so we tented nearby.

Day 20—Sunday, April 10, 2011

We got a late start, as we began hiking at 9:00. The trail ascended about 1,200 feet in the first four miles. By late morning, we saw a sign indicating that a side trail led to Clingmans Dome (6,643 ft.), the highest point on the AT. Swamp Dawg had previously gone up the observation tower there, so he decided to rest while I climbed to get a 360-degree view of the park. Mount LeConte was a striking sight in the distance.

As I began my walk back to the AT, I saw a couple just a few steps ahead of me. The man was wearing an Ohio State baseball cap. I said hello and told the couple that I was from Ohio and was thru-hiking the AT. The man knew the AT was nearby, but he didn't know exactly where it was. I told him that I would show him. He and his wife followed me down the side trail to where Swamp Dawg was resting. The woman asked if she could take a picture of me with her husband. After the photo, the man took a few steps on the trail. He said, "Now I can tell my family that I hiked on the AT and got a photo with a thru-hiker from Ohio to prove it as well." After I shook hands with the couple, Swamp Dawg and I resumed our hike.

We reached the Mt. Collins Shelter (5,870 ft.) at 3:45. Although we had hiked only 10 miles on the sunny day, we decided to stay there because the next shelter was more than seven miles ahead. It was a real treat to have a leisurely afternoon. I hung my damp clothes to dry over branches of bushes next to the shelter. A little while later, two hikers (Tony and Scrap) arrived. Tony did not have a trail name at that point.   Since the shelter was designed to sleep 14, everyone had plenty of room to spread out their sleeping bag and gear.

Day 21—Monday, April 11, 2011

After hiking almost five miles, we took a break at Newfound Gap (U.S. 441). It is the only road access on the AT within the Smokies. Many hikers hitch a ride from there into Gatlinburg, Tennessee, to resupply and enjoy its many attractions. Swamp Dawg had previously convinced me to carry enough food in order not to have to leave the trail there. Over the next hour, Swamp Dawg and I stopped a few times for him to rest. At one break, he said that I should continue on, and he would catch up with me. I reluctantly went ahead alone.

About a half-hour later, a south-bound hiker approached. I stopped and spoke with him. I told him about Swamp Dawg's health problem and what he was wearing. I reached into my pack and pulled out a Snickers bar. I gave it to the hiker to give to Swamp Dawg. I knew from experience that a Snickers bar gave me an energy boost while hiking. I hoped it would do the same for him.

When I reached the Icewater Spring Shelter (5,920 ft.), I stopped for lunch. Swamp Dawg had not arrived at the shelter by early afternoon, so I decided to write him a note in the shelter register. I told him that I was heading to Peck's Corner Shelter (5,280 ft.), which was about seven miles ahead. Just as I was about to leave, Swamp Dawg arrived. He thanked me for sending him the candy bar via the south-bound hiker. He thought that his problem of fatigue was due to high blood pressure. He was considering hiking back three miles to Newfound Gap to hitch a ride into Gatlinburg to see a doctor. He told me that I should continue hiking without him. He said that if I stayed with him, I would likely not finish the thru-hike.

Swamp Dawg suggested that he might be able to catch up with me by slack-packing. A slackpacker usually carries only the essentials of food and water needed for a day hike. A hostel owner will shuttle a slackpacker to a drop-off point near the trail and pick him up at the end of the day at a prearranged destination. After spending the night at the hostel, the hiker is returned to the trail the following morning to the place where he last hiked. A slackpacker carries far less weight, experiences less fatigue, and is capable of hiking a greater distance than he would by carrying the weight of a full backpack, including tent, sleeping bag, clothes, and perhaps several days of food. Although some frown on slackpacking, it is very popular with many hikers. Most hikers take great effort to keep their pack weight down. A slackpacker does the same thing, simply carried to the extreme. One slackpacker said to me, "I'm out here on the AT to hike and enjoy the wilderness. I am not here to carry more weight than I have to during the hike."

I felt terrible about Swamp Dawg as his problem had become my problem. After twelve great days of hiking together, I reluctantly agreed to move on without him and hike alone again. I certainly didn't expect to find another wonderful hiker like him to share my journey. I gave Swamp Dawg a hug at the shelter and with tears in my eyes, I turned and headed north on the trail. I thought about Swamp Dawg with a heavy heart the rest of the day. In less than a mile, I passed the boulder-like protruding rock formation called Charlies Bunion (5,905 ft.), a popular spot for day hikers to visit. The mountain has a bare-rock summit, which is a rare sight in the Smokies. By the late afternoon I reached Peck's Corner Shelter (5,280 ft.). I had hiked about 15 miles. I was pleased that the shelter was full, so I could sleep in my tent for the third time in the Smokies.

Day 22—Tuesday, April 12, 2011—Week 4

In the morning, it was cold and rainy. That turned out to be the best part of the day. The temperature continued to drop, and a biting wind was accompanied by snow and hail. I wore gloves and put on my knitted hat to cover my head and ears. It was the worst weather I experienced on my entire hike.

I stopped at the Tri-Corner Shelter (5,920 ft.) for a snack in mid-morning. I met a hiker there named Lost, a 49-year old accountant from the Seattle, Washington area. Lost may have done more hiking in recent years than accounting work. He had finished two impressive thru-hikes—the Pacific Crest Trail (PCT) and the Continental Divide Trail. He was hoping to thru-hike the AT and complete the "triple crown of hiking."

Lost left the shelter and began hiking a few minutes before I did. However, it didn't take me long to catch up with and then pass him. My hands were very cold, so I tried to generate body heat by hiking at the fastest pace I could. I certainly didn't have to worry about breaking sweat in the frigid temperature. No one passed me over the next few hours of hiking.

After hiking nearly 13 miles in inclement weather, I saw a welcome sight, the Cosby Knob Shelter (4,700 ft.). The shelters in the Smokies used to have screened-in front entrances to keep out bears. Many years ago, the front of each shelter was equipped instead with a large tarp to keep out the wind. It was determined that the wind presented a bigger problem for hikers in the shelters than bears. About 2:30, I entered the shelter by pulling back the tarp and found several hikers already nestled into their sleeping bags.

The shelter had space for six hikers to sleep on each of two levels. The bottom level was already full, so I climbed a short ladder to the top. Soon Tony, Scrap, and Lost arrived. I mentioned to Tony that I hoped I could sleep in the confined space of the shelter. I expected that snorers would probably wake me up. I was envious of Tony because he maintained that snorers would not cause a problem for him.

The shelter was full within an hour as the last few spots were taken. I felt really sorry for several hikers that arrived later. They learned there was no place to

A shelter in the Smokies with a tarp over the front

sleep in the shelter. I heard two men say they'd push on to the next shelter. I would have hated to hike another seven miles in that cold and windy weather to the next shelter. I would not have traded places with any of those distressed hikers even for a large amount of money. After I put on my long underwear, it took me about a half hour simply to get warm in my 30-degree-rated sleeping bag. It was the coldest I got on the entire hike.

Day 23—Wednesday, April 13, 2011

It was chilly in the morning, but it wasn't raining, snowing, or hailing. The wind had greatly diminished, and eventually it turned into a pleasant day. As I was hiking, I thought of the snoring I had heard the night before. It wasn't so bad as to awaken me from a sound sleep, but I did recall hearing some. As I thought of Tony who maintained that he was never bothered by the snoring of others, I thought of a trail name for him— "Sleep Tight."

After a descent of over 2,700 feet covering eight miles, I approached the road at Davenport Gap, the eastern boundary of the GSMNP about noon. Within a few yards of the road several hikers, including Tony, were standing and eating. I told Tony about my trail name for him. He liked it, and from then on he was known as Sleep Tight!

35

The hikers were enjoying trail magic provided by three women and a man. It was truly a real feast! The friendly group of four said that several times each spring they offered lunch to thru-hikers at Davenport Gap. They seemed as happy in providing the food and beverage treat as hikers were in getting it. The group said that the park made it difficult to offer trail magic at Newfound Gap, the only other road access on the AT in the Smokies. Park Rangers told the group that they needed to obtain a license and liability insurance in order to feed hikers in the GSMNP. However, the road at Davenport Gap was just outside the park, where there was no such regulation. As I was leaving, a woman in the group put a banana and apple under the netting on my backpack, so I had a healthy snack for later.

The AT crosses the road at Davenport Gap, marking the border between Tennessee and North Carolina. At that point, TN 32 is a paved road that goes north, while NC 284 is an unpaved road that goes south.

It had taken me over five days to hike the 72-mile trek through the GSMNP. I felt blessed that I had experienced mostly dry mild weather in early April with only one difficult day of hiking. The weather can be very rough in the Smokies in early spring. When Swamp Dawg had hiked through the park in early April several years before, the snow was knee high.

NORTH CAROLINA & TENNESSEE BORDER

Over the next 152 miles, the AT skirted the border of North Carolina and Tennessee. I would be in one state for a short time and then in the other. After hiking about 10 miles, I reached the Green Corner Road in Hartford, Tennessee, about 2:30. I walked several hundred yards down a gravel road to the Standing Bear Farm Hiker Hostel.

I chose to stay in the rustic bunkhouse. I washed my clothes with a scrub board before putting them through an old-fashion ringer to remove excess water. I felt like an early pioneer until I put the damp clothes into a dryer—a modern convenience! I rinsed my ground cover and rain fly for my tent in the stream that ran right through the property. I hung them to dry over the railing of a small foot bridge covering the stream.

Kebban was at the hostel and bunked near me. He dealt with a perilous situation in the Smokies. He was hiking with a British woman, and he offered to take her picture at Charlies Bunion. When she offered to reciprocate, he stepped back from her and fell precariously close to the edge of a cliff. He injured his ribs in the fall and was in pain. His camera dropped from his hand and fell a long distance, crashing down onto rocks well below. It was impossible to retrieve. Kebban had taken a lot of photos, and with one misstep, everything was lost. I realized how quickly a positive situation on the trail could turn negative or even disastrous. It was a good reminder to be observant, watching out for dangerous situations.

Day 24—Thursday, April 14, 2011

As I was getting ready to leave the hostel in the morning, a van arrived with several hikers. To my surprise, Swamp Dawg was one of them. It was great to see him, and we talked for a few minutes. He was feeling better than when I had last seen him just three days before. We agreed to meet at Trail Days in mid-May.

I left the hostel at 9:30. The trail ascended nearly 2,500 feet over the next several hours. After I summited Snowbird Mountain (4,263 ft.), there was 1,400-foot descent. Then I climbed 1,800 feet to the summit of Max Patch (4,629 feet), which was forested before early settlers cleared the top of the mountain for live-stock to graze. The U.S. Forest Service now maintains the bald appearance by mowing and using controlled burns. The summit covers nearly 400 acres and provides spectacular views in every direction. I reached the Roaring Fork Shelter (3,950 ft.) about 6:15 and camped nearby. I felt blessed for having had such a great day, and my spirit was lifted. I visited with Swamp Dawg, hiked over 15 miles in good weather, and saw some fantastic sights.

Day 25—Friday, April 15, 2011

I was on the trail early determined to reach Hot Springs, NC, the first town located on the AT. I needed to hike 18 miles—my longest hike to date. Thankfully, the terrain was relatively easy. The last eight miles of the hike were down-hill, descending 3,300 feet from Bluff Mountain (4,686 ft.). In the late afternoon, the trail reached the outskirts of Hot Springs (population 635). I turned left on Bridge Street and headed toward the center of the town. There were diamond designs in the sidewalk to mark the trail. This attention to detail was ample evidence that Hot Springs was a friendly trail town.

I stopped first at the famous Sunnybank Inn, a white Victorian house set back off the street. Elmer Hall has owned and run the inn for many years. I really wanted to stay there, as I had heard about the wonderful organic vegetarian meals that it offers. Unfortunately, the inn was full. I walked a short distance to the L & K Deli and bought a soda and snack. I was sitting on a bench near the street enjoying a break, when Kebban appeared. He had wanted to stay at Elmer's too. After I told him that the inn was full, we began to walk together through town.

In a few minutes, I saw a young hiker named Red Blaze, whom I had last seen at Fontana Dam. He was standing in a parking lot, talking with a young woman and several other hikers. He said, "Would you guys like some free food?" Now that really caught my attention and drew my interest. Food is the number one topic of conversation on the AT, and Red Blaze had just added the magic word "free."

Red Blaze introduced his twin sister, Allie, who had started to hike with him in Georgia. Shortly after the start, she broke her ankle and left the trail. Allie had a large amount of food that she had planned to have shipped to her along the trail. She no longer needed it and chose to give it away to thru-hikers. Wow! Here was another example of trail magic! Kebban and I each took several dehydrated dinners, energy bars, and snack items. In effect, we had resupplied for free. We thanked Allie and moved on, appreciative of being at the right place at the right time.

Kebban decided to pay for a camping spot at the Hot Springs Campground near the north end of town. I thought seriously of joining him. However, I had seen a posted sign coming into town that stated hikers could stay for free that weekend at an area just off the trail on the northern outskirts of town. I liked the offer of free camping, so I kept going. To get there, I continued walking through town, crossing the railroad tracks. I continued over the French Broad River Bridge. Then I climbed over the guardrail at the north end of the bridge and walked down the embankment. I continued along the road, past where the AT branched off. When I reached the camping area, I was surprised to find that I was the only camper there. Perhaps no other hiker could find the site!

As I entered town, I had seen a notice promoting an AYCE lasagna dinner for $10 at the Senior Community Center from 6-8 p.m. After I set my tent, I headed into town to eat. After dinner, as I headed back to my campsite, it started to rain lightly. Soon it began to rain harder, and I hurried to get into my tent. I wished then that I had gotten a place to stay with a roof over my head. The free camping spot had lost some of its appeal!

Day 26—Saturday, April 16, 2011

By morning the rain had ceased, and I headed back into town. I stopped at an outfitter to buy a butane fuel canister for my stove. Then I went to eat breakfast at the Smoky Mountain Diner. I met Kebban there, and he told another harrowing story. As he slept at the Hot Springs Campground, a large tree fell very near his tent. If his tent had been slightly closer to the tree, he may have been struck by the falling timber.

Kebban's story made me think of a sobering thought. I could have stayed at the Hot Springs Campground and set up my tent near his. In that case, the tree could have landed on my tent, and I would not have been eating breakfast that morning in the diner. I thought of how the posted notice that led me to the free camping site may have saved my life. Up to that point on the hike, I had seen a lot of Kebban. However, that day was the last time that I saw him. Many months later, I heard that he had experienced foot problems that caused him to end his dream of thru-hiking the AT in 2011.

After breakfast, I walked back to my campsite and took down my wet tent. I realized that since I had entered Hot Springs, I had walked several miles going to and from town. Unfortunately, none of those miles got me any closer to my goal of thru-hiking the AT.

I experienced the strangest day weather-wise on the trail. After I began hiking, it started raining lightly. As the rain ended, it became sunny and nice. A few hours later, it got cloudy with a slight breeze. Then the wind picked up, and it got much colder.

I had climbs totaling well over 3,000 feet by mid-afternoon. By late afternoon I had hiked 11 miles and was happy to camp at the Spring Mountain Shelter (3,300 ft.). I thought of how the terrain and weather had directly affected the distance I hiked. The 11-mile trek was much more difficult than the 18-mile hike the day before.

Day 27—Sunday, April 17, 2011

At 6:15 I was awakened by the howl of a coyote. However, the coyote wasn't nearly as close as the one that seemed to be right next to my tent 12 days earlier. I wasn't eager to get started hiking, as the temperature hovered near 30 degrees. I finally mustered the courage to get going about 8:45. By 10:30 the sun had come out, and it turned into a lovely day in the Cherokee National Forest.

Soon I met two south-bound section hikers from Michigan. They had stopped to get water out of a creek. I decided to do the same. While I was in a crouched position straddling the creek, I realized that the water wasn't very clean. As I moved to get up and not take the water there, I fell to one side. Both of my feet went into the water, and my pants got wet to about my knees. Thankfully, my backpack didn't go under the water. I stumbled out of the creek, embarrassed and wet. I imagine the hikers thought that I wouldn't complete my thru-hike and would be lucky not to drown on the trail. I decided not to change my pants, as I expected the warming temperature and my body heat to dry them by the time I camped.

The longest ascent of the day was over 2,500 feet from Allen Gap (2,234 ft.) to Camp Creek Bald Mountain (4,750 ft.). In the late afternoon, I encountered Blackstack Cliffs (4,420 ft.), a very rugged and difficult area with treacherous ascents and descents over large boulders. Only a very narrow path existed as I maneuvered through the cliffs. My backpack and body often brushed the rocks or foliage on both sides. What a relief to get through that area and back to a normal trail! By 6:15 I had hiked nearly 16 miles and set up camp at the Jerry Cabin Shelter (4,150 ft.).

Day 28—Monday, April 18, 2011

The weather in the morning was ideal for hiking with the temperature in the 50-degree range. I laughed when I saw the name of the first mountain to climb for the day—Big Butt (4,750 ft.)! I hiked most of the day with Lost, whom I had met in the Smokies. Lost demonstrated to me where to position my hiking sticks to utilize a minimum amount of arm movement. He claimed that his technique would conserve energy, while generating the maximum amount of forward movement. He laughed when I thanked him for sharing with me "The Lost Theory of Hiking Techniques!"

The day went quickly with an ongoing conversation between Lost and me. We talked about our lives and our past experiences. I realized how different we were. He had completed two very long-distance hikes while I had completed just 300 miles of my first long-distance hike. He had never been married and had no children. I had been married 43 years with two daughters and five grandchildren. He had no source of regular income and relied on his girlfriend to help finance his hike. I had a comfortable retirement, and my wife was a stay-at-home mom until our daughters left the nest. He was 49, and I was 67— a difference of 18 years. I had never been in the state of Washington while he had never been in Ohio.

After hiking nearly 15 miles, I reached the Hogback Ridge Shelter (4,255 ft.) and decided to set up my tent. Lost took a short break before continuing to hike, looking to find just the right campsite. He needed to be situated between two trees, so that he could hang his hammock. He hung a tarp over a line above it to keep dry in case of rain. He also liked the peace and quiet of camping alone. In the south there were numerous spots along the trail that met both of those conditions.

Day 29—Tuesday, April 19, 2011—Week 5

I began a long day of hiking at 7:00. I had ascents totaling 3,400 feet and descents totaling 4,300 feet. The high point of the day was the 360-degree view on Big Bald Mountain (5,516 feet). Although the Southern Appalachians do not rise above tree line, there are many balds or treeless summits. There are various theories of the origins of some of the balds. One is that the harsh conditions at high elevations were responsible. Others theorize that Native Americans cleared the mountain for religious ceremonies, or perhaps the balds resulted from animal grazing and crop planting.

Along the trail, I began to see Mountain Laurel bushes, which have a bowl or cup-shaped, pink-to-white flower in large clusters. After hiking over 11 hours, I arrived at the No Business Knob Shelter (3,180 ft.) just after 6:00. I had set a new personal record, as I hiked nearly 21 miles. I thought of how hiking 10 miles or less in a day was now considered a short hike. Earlier, I would have considered a 10-mile hike a long distance.

Day 30—Wednesday, April 20, 2011

I began hiking very early in order to arrive before 9:00 at the Nolichucky Hostel in Erwin, Tennessee. I wanted to take advantage of the hostel's free shuttle to a restaurant for breakfast. After I awoke about 4:30, I took down my tent and packed my gear in darkness. I looked like a coal miner wearing a headlamp as I started slowly inching down the trail slightly before 6:00. My hiking sticks prevented me from falling a few minutes later. I began to doubt my sanity for hiking in the dark. Soon I encountered a huge tree that had blown down, completely obstructing the trail. There was no good way to get around it. I decided to climb over and under its branches, sometimes on all fours. As I was feeling battered and bruised by the branches, I wondered if the tree had taken delight in abusing me. Back on the normal trail, I had a new worry. I tried to downplay the thought that something may have fallen out of my pack or pocket while I was on the ground desperately trying to get past the fallen tree. It took about a half-hour of hiking in the dark before dawn arrived. At that moment, I decided that I had enough of night hiking and never wanted to do it again!

At 8:00 I could see Erwin (population 6,097) below in the distance.

Looking down at Erwin, TN

Coming down the mountain, the trail descended to River Road. From there I turned left, and a minute later I reached the Nolichucky Hostel at 8:40. I had hiked over six miles. The Nolichucky Hostel is owned by John Shores and is simply known as Uncle Johnny's Hostel. I had enough time to secure a bunk and unload my gear before boarding a van to be shuttled to breakfast at J. D.'s Market and Deli. It was not exactly a five-star restaurant, but shuttled hikers can't be choosers! There were six stools at a counter. Thankfully the food was much better than the ambiance.

After breakfast, the van returned and picked me up, along with a load of hikers. The driver stopped at the Post Office. One hiker got a box of dehydrated food from home that had not been properly prepared and was moldy. He did not relish telling his mother of the problem because he knew it would upset her. Since it was actually the second time that mold was prevalent, he had no choice but to give her the bad news before she shipped another box.

After I returned to the hostel, I saw Lost and several other hikers who had arrived too late to get the 9:00 shuttle to breakfast. I did my laundry before the shuttle left again about noon to take a load of hikers, including me, to an AYCE pizza shop for lunch. In the early evening, I had arranged to meet a local couple (Ken Kisiel and Judy King). Ken's sister is Shelly Mack from Berea, whom I had known for years. After Ken and Judy took me to dinner at a Mexican restaurant, I resupplied at a supermarket. Ken and Judy's hospitality was another example of trail magic. At the end of the day, I was quite pleased to have enjoyed three meals at restaurants, and I reflected on memories of my first 30 days on the trail.

Day 31—Thursday, April 21, 2011

When I left Uncle Johnny's Hostel (1,700 ft.) in the morning, the weather was spectacular. In the early afternoon, I hiked over Unaka Mountain (5,180 ft.), the highest elevation of the day. I had ascents totaling over 3,800 feet. By late afternoon, I had hiked about 17 miles when I reached the Cherry Gap Shelter (3,900 ft.) and set up camp. As I ate dinner at the picnic table, a hiker was eating peanut butter and Nutella on a bagel. He said he really enjoyed the creamy chocolate taste of Nutella. His positive remarks about it convinced me to buy a jar in the future.

Day 32—Friday, April 22, 2011

In the morning, I had to take my tent down in the rain. Fortunately, the rain was really a very light mist. The day soon turned cloudy, colder, and windy. While descending the trail, I fell on wet leaves covering slippery mud, but I wasn't hurt. Moments later, I almost went down again. My hiking sticks saved me from a fall that time, as they had done numerous times before and after. I remember that Swamp Dawg said he would rather forego his tent than his hiking sticks. I would agree! The hiking sticks helped to pull me forward on ascents, yet they were most valuable for balance and support on descents. They prevented me from descending too fast and helped me achieve a safe landing in areas littered with rocks and roots.

In the afternoon, I passed the Roan High Knob Shelter (6,275 feet), the highest on the AT. Roan Mountain is the last time that the AT climbs above 6,000 feet until New Hampshire. The long day featured rocky and difficult climbs, and one hiker called the climb up Roan Mountain the "Stairway to Heaven." In addition, Roan Mountain is said to be arguably the coldest spot throughout the year on the southern AT.

When I reached Carver's Gap (5,512 ft.), the weather got really nasty, and the terrain got tougher. The wind and snow flakes made each step a challenge. I was still slightly over three miles from my destination, and I became concerned that I may not reach it before dark. After 12 hours on the trail, I finally made it to the Stan Murray Shelter (5,050 ft.) at 7:15. I quickly set up my tent and ate a bagel with peanut butter and jelly.

As I reviewed the day, I was pleased. I had hiked over 20 miles on a nasty day with ascents totaling nearly 3,700 feet. I snuggled into my sleeping bag on the windiest night I experienced on the entire hike. My tent was staked down on all corners, and as usual, I had all my gear with me inside the tent. Still, I was hoping and praying that the tent would stay upright and remain in one piece as the wind seemed to beat on it violently. Throughout the night, a flapping noise continued, which could have kept a restless sleeper awake all night. However, as tired as I was, it barely disturbed me.

Day 33—Saturday, April 23, 2011

In the morning, I got water from a spring on a blue-blazed trail opposite the shelter. I reveled in the fact that I didn't have to treat it with Aqua Mira. I usually got water when I reached a shelter at the end of a day. However, I had put off that chore the night before because darkness had set in. As I started hiking at 7:00, it was cold. Fortunately, the wind had died down. After I had been on the trail for a short time, the sun came out.

I stopped to adjust my pack and take off my jacket as Lost came down the trail. After we spoke briefly, he continued hiking. Several minutes later, I saw Lost again when I went by him as he was eating a snack just off the trail. Passing a hiker and then in turn being passed by that same hiker often occurs several times in one day.

By mid-morning I reached Bradley Gap (4,950 ft.). I stopped and took a photo of the sign because I thought of my young grandson, Bradley Schuster, the son of my younger daughter, Michelle, and her husband, Bob. Soon I hiked over Hump Mountain (5,587 ft.) and then stopped for a break. The instep on my right foot was bothering me. The problem was caused by my boot laces being too tight. I loosened them and cut a strip of moleskin to place over the hot spot that had turned red.

As I was finishing my efforts to solve my foot problem, a hiker named Torch greeted me. He had been called Torch beginning in high school, when a teammate on the track team said he resembled a flaming torch as he ran around the oval with his red hair blowing in the breeze. It was hard for me to imagine as Torch was now bald. We had a lot in common as we both grew up in Northeast Ohio and had graduated from Kent State University.

I hiked with Torch for about an hour when we happily discovered trail magic. A couple had set up a table with plenty of food and sodas. After 20 minutes of enjoying their hospitality, we resumed hiking and reached U.S. 19E about 1:00. We turned left on the highway and walked .3 of a mile down the road to the highly recommended Mountain Harbour B & B and Hostel, owned by Mary and Tracy Hill.

The hostel is in the upstairs of a barn and overlooks a creek with a few goats meandering around. Mary told me that the goats keep the grass down, and as a result, snakes are less likely to be in that area. A horse was in the corral, which was attached to the barn. The B & B was just up the knoll. About 5:00, Tracy drove a load of hikers, including me, to resupply at the Dollar General and then to a restaurant for supper. When we returned, I folded my clean clothes that Mary had washed.

Day 34—Sunday, April 24, 2011

It was Easter Sunday, the joyous day that Jesus Christ rose from the dead. The breakfast that Mary prepared was as good as or better than any that I had ever eaten at a restaurant. The quantity and quality of food was mind boggling. In fact, even after several plates, I had not tried all the delicious items she had prepared. My mouth waters even now when I think of it!

TENNESSEE

I had completed the AT in two states (GA & NC) with 12 states to go. I set out about 9:00 to begin hiking 71 miles through Tennessee. Later in the morning, the trail came to a large rock. Halfway around it, the trail appeared to veer to the right. I followed the well-worn path, which eventually stopped abruptly in about a quarter mile. Some previous hikers who had made the same mistake I had made had led me astray, so I retraced my steps to the large rock. Upon closer review, I saw that the white blaze indicated the trail went around the rock and then straight ahead through some underbrush. I was unhappy having lost about 15 minutes of time and having walked about a half mile out of my way, but I was relieved to be back on the trail.

After the fantastic five-star breakfast at the hostel, I figured that I may not have to eat again for several days. Of course, as good as Mary Hill's food was, that thought vanished sometime in the afternoon. Eating a bagel with cheese was a far cry from the scrumptious breakfast I enjoyed. At 5:45 I completed hiking about 16 miles and camped just off the trail.

Day 35—Monday, April 25, 2011

I began hiking shortly before 7:00. I had a steep climb of 1,900 feet and two descents of 1,800 and 2,100 feet. The highest elevation of the day was at White Rocks Mountain (4,206 ft.). I began to see a huge number of beautiful butterflies and bumblebees. Their frequent appearance continued over the next two weeks. My appetite was becoming voracious, so at every break, I began eating snack crackers or a candy bar.

In the early afternoon, I came to beautiful Laurel Fork Falls, the largest waterfall on the AT.

Laurel Fork Falls, TN

As I walked along the water, a snake met me on the narrow trail. After it posed for me to take its picture, I poked one of my hiking sticks at it to get it to move off the trail. The serpent had the foolish idea that I should be the one who moved out of its way. Instead of moving, it struck twice at my stick. Then it got in a coiled position and struck a third time. Realizing that its actions were not having the desired effect, the snake turned and began to move away. Using one of my sticks, I flicked it into the water.

As the day was ending, I reached Watauga Lake and passed people picnicking along the shore. Just before 6:30, I staggered into the Watauga Lake Shelter (2,130 ft.). Several hikers were sitting at the picnic table drinking beer. I knew many of them, including Moosehead, Orange Blaze, Porter, and Pace. It had been a warm day, and I had hiked over 19 miles. I sat at the end of the picnic table and enjoyed several cold beers, courtesy of Porter and Pace. Although I am not a big beer drinker, the cold beverages were refreshing after a long day of hiking.

Day 36—Tuesday, April 26, 2011—Week 6

I began hiking at 6:30. During the day, I saw a box tortoise in the middle of the trail. It reminded me of one I found as a young child. I named that one, Myrtle the Turtle. After a week as my pet, I put Myrtle in the backyard to enjoy the sunshine as I figured she wouldn't go far. After a half-hour, I began to look for her, but Myrtle had disappeared! I learned that a tortoise could move faster than I had imagined. Now about 60 years later, I thought that perhaps the tortoise on the trail in Tennessee was a descendant of Myrtle. Over the next several weeks, I saw a similar one on the trail about three times. Each time I thought of Myrtle the Turtle!

The degree of difficulty for the day was only moderate, but there was a 2,000-foot ascent. The highest elevation of the day was in the afternoon, when I passed by the Iron Mountain Shelter (4,125 ft.). At 5:00 just after getting water out of a stream, I camped right off the trail. I had hiked over 17 miles.

Day 37—Wednesday, April 27, 2011

I began hiking just before 7:00 on a really nice day. Hiking was easy with only moderate ascents and descents. The highest elevation of the day was in the morning as I passed by Double Springs Shelter (4,060 ft.).

VIRGINIA

In the afternoon, I saw the sign that marked the Tennessee/Virginia border. Three states down (GA, NC, and TN) and eleven states to go! The AT winds 550 miles through Virginia—the longest distance by far of any state on the AT. Since about 25% of the AT is in Virginia, I expected to be in the state for more than a month. From the border, the trail descends about 1,400 feet in less than four miles into Damascus (population 814), which I reached about 4:30. It has the reputation of being the friendliest town on the AT. I had hiked over 22 miles, a new personal record.

I had planned to stay at The Place, a church hostel in Damascus. However, as I reached the center of town, I met Lost walking toward me on the sidewalk. He had rented a small room with two beds at a hostel called Dave's Place just across the street. I accepted Lost's offer to share the cost of the room with him.

A hiker told us that a local man would pick up hikers at the gazebo in town at 6:00 and take them to his home for supper. That sounded great! We waited there until 6:15. We were ready to leave when a pick-up truck finally arrived. We got into the bed of the truck with two other hikers and were driven about five minutes to an old farm house in the country. When we arrived, I was surprised to see about 15 hikers and several goats and piglets on the property. There was enough food to have served even more hikers. Most of us donated $5 to offset the cost of the family's hospitality. We were driven back to the gazebo in town after dinner. What a great a day I had!

Day 38—Thursday, April 28, 2011

In the morning, electric power was out in a wide area. As Lost and I walked to breakfast, we stopped at two restaurants, but they were both closed. We finally saw a convenience store of a service station that was open, but only for cash transactions. The storm had been quite severe as a tornado had hit nearby, killing several people and destroying many buildings.

I had planned to take a zero day to buy a new sleeping bag, go to the Post Office, resupply, and check my e-mail at the library. As I came back from breakfast, I saw that the library was closed. I wondered whether the rest of the businesses I planned to visit would be open. I was pleased that the outfitter was! The front windows of the store provided enough light to see the merchandise. I bought an emergency sleeping bag, which was intended as a replacement for my 30-degree sleeping bag. Since it was nearly May, I did not think I needed such a warm one with summer around the corner. The new bag was thin, shiny silver, and manufactured from the same thermal-reflective film in emergency blankets. Those ultra-light blankets have been called space blankets and are used by runners to stay warm after completing a long-distance-running event. I thought my idea was brilliant—a stroke of genius. I would be able to reduce weight and save space in my backpack with the new sleeping bag. The outfitter took my credit card number to charge my purchase when power was restored.

Just before noon, I walked to the Post Office. I was lucky that it was still open, but only for ten more minutes. The Post Office, like the convenience store, accepted only cash as payment. I sent my 30-degree sleeping bag home. I also bounced a box containing some items that I thought I may want later to the Wood's Hole Hostel and Mountain Retreat near Pearisburg, Virginia.

Then I walked a half mile to the supermarket, which I had heard was open. A sign was posted on the doors of the refrigerated cases in the store that stated, "Don't open!" Dry ice was in each case. I was surprised that the supermarket did not have a backup generator. However, I did not want to buy any refrigerated items, so the restriction did not affect me. I bought Nutella for the first time. I thought that if I liked it, I would use it on a bagel with peanut butter in place of jelly. Instead of PB and J, I would have PB and N.

Although rain threatened the whole day, it remained dry. I had the same opportunity to go to the farm house, where the free meal had been served the previous evening. The new menu included a turkey and dressing dinner. Although the menu sounded excellent, I decided to save time and stay at the hostel. I ate some of the food that I had just bought earlier in the day. As I thought about the storm, I realized that the tornado only caused me minor inconveniences compared to others nearby. Thankfully the tornado did not hit Damascus. I said a prayer for those poor people just 10 miles away who were much less fortunate.

Day 39—Friday, April 29, 2011

While I was asleep, the power was restored. In the morning, I weighed myself. I was startled that my weight had dropped to 143 pounds, the lowest I had weighed since high school. I had begun the hike at 163 pounds. My percentage of weight loss though was 12%, which was similar to other male hikers that I knew.

I resumed hiking at 7:45 on a dry morning. The longest climb was about 1,000 feet right after leaving Damascus. During the day, there were ascents totaling about 3,300 feet. I felt beat and took a 15-minute rest mid-day at the Saunders Shelter (3,310 ft.). After hiking nearly 16 miles, I reached the Lost Mountain Shelter (3,360 ft.) at 4:30. I laughed when I thought that perhaps Lost Mountain and the Lost Mountain Shelter were named in honor of my hiking friend, Lost. After I set up my tent and secured water, I enjoyed relaxing the rest of the day.

Day 40—Saturday, April 30, 2011

In the morning, I was not a happy camper as condensation had developed inside my sleeping bag overnight. It was as if someone had sprinkled water inside.

My clothes were quite damp. The new bag didn't breathe, and condensation had resulted from my warm body inside and the cold temperature on the outside.

I began to hike about 6:45 in good weather. The trail was very rugged and rocky with ascents totaling over 3,200 feet. The longest climb was nearly 1,600 feet to Buzzard Rock on Whitetop Mountain (5,080 ft.). On a positive note, the difficult ascents were rewarded with breathtaking views from the mountain tops. The highest elevation of the day was Rhododendron Gap (5,440 ft.).

Late in the afternoon, I saw wild horses in Grayson Highlands State Park (4,460 ft.). I had heard that the feral ponies would often eat out of a hiker's hand, but no horses showed any interest in me. I wondered if it may have been because I smelled so bad that even wild horses didn't want to be near me! It was just as well as I really didn't want horse saliva on my hands. I hiked until 6:00 and completed over 17 miles. I set up my tent near the trail in a nice flat area.

Day 41—Sunday, May 1, 2011

While I slept, condensation inside my sleeping bag continued to be a major problem. I realized that my stroke of shining brilliance was more of a disastrous deed of dumbness. I was not as smart as I thought. I shouldn't have sent my 30-degree bag home until I was sure I had a decent replacement.

I began my hike once again at 6:45. I called Cindi in the morning and asked her to send back my sleeping bag to a hostel, where I planned to be in about a week. The highlight of the day was seeing long-horn steers with horns that were several feet long. I was alert as I walked within five feet of the steers, but they showed no sign of aggression. The day of hiking was pretty easy. The highest elevation was Pine Mountain (5,000 ft.).

About 3:30, I reached Dickey Gap (3,300 ft.) at VA 650. A man was standing there talking to two hikers, who were resting on the ground. After I said hello and walked by, I started to hitch a ride into Troutdale, Virginia (population 178). The man immediately asked me if I wanted a ride in his old Volkswagen van into Troutdale, and I gladly accepted. His name was Gary, and he was accompanied by his dog, Pepper. Gary and Pepper had hiked the trail previously. Gary was a trail angel, like Red Hat in North Carolina. He dropped me off a few miles up the road at Jerry's Kitchen. I accepted his offer to meet me at again about 8:00 the next morning at the restaurant to drive me two miles back to the AT.

At Jerry's Kitchen, I ordered pizza and a chocolate milk shake for dinner. It was the best milk shake I ever drank—made with several scoops of ice cream, a lot of chocolate sauce, and just the right amount of milk. The restaurant had one computer available for customers to use, so I checked my e-mail. Then I walked down the road about a quarter mile to the Troutdale Baptist Church Hostel. There was a bathroom about 50 yards away from the bunkhouse, where I enjoyed a hot shower. Since it was only early evening, I hung my damp things on a clothes line outside the hostel. Surprisingly, I had the comfortable, enclosed bunkhouse to myself. I had hiked 16 miles during the nine-hour day.

Day 42—Monday, May 2, 2011

In the morning, I walked back to Jerry's Kitchen when it opened at 7:00, and I enjoyed a wonderful breakfast. It was early May, and the weather was beautiful. Gary and Pepper appeared about 8:15 to drive me back to the AT. I gave Gary $5 for gas money and thanked him for his help.

After hiking 14 easy miles, I arrived at the Partnership Shelter about 3:45. The large shelter sleeps 16 and is equipped with a propane-powered warm-water shower. The shelter is just a short walk from the Mount Rogers National Recreational Center at VA 16. I expected to order a pizza and have it delivered to the gate there. Instead, I was met with a nice surprise.

When I arrived, there were about five hikers at the shelter, including Lost. I had last seen him three days before. One of the hikers, whom I met for the first time, was Portrait. He had a large camera and enjoyed taking photos on the trail. He carried a custom-made backpack, which looked like plastic grocery bags sewn together. He had very few clothes, and his tent was extremely light weight. The most amazing thing was that, even with his heavy camera, his entire pack weighed only about 18 pounds.

It was Portrait's 30th birthday, and he wanted to celebrate his big day with fellow thru-hikers. Shortly before I arrived, Portrait had hiked several miles into a town and bought a birthday cake, paper plates, utensils, chips, small fruit pies, and a Styrofoam cooler to hold a five-gallon tub of ice cream and sodas. As Portrait was paying for the merchandise, the cashier asked him if he was going to a party. Portrait explained his situation. The cashier was ending his shift and kindly offered Portrait a ride back to near the shelter. Portrait celebrated his birthday with lucky hikers like me at the Partnership Shelter. It was the only birthday party I experienced on the trail. After eating cake, ice cream, pie, chips, and drinking two sodas, I did not need to order a pizza.

It was only 4:30 as the party wound down. The rest of the hikers, including Lost, spent the night at the shelter, but I decided to continue hiking. It was the last time that I saw Lost on the AT. I hiked for three more hours until 7:30. I set up camp 40 feet off the trail, just past U.S. Forest Service Road 644. I was pleased to have gone to a great birthday party and still have hiked 22 miles.

Day 43—Tuesday, May 3, 2011—Week 7

I began hiking on an empty stomach just before 7:00. I knew that in about four miles the trail went right through Atkins, Virginia. I planned to eat a big breakfast there at the Barn Restaurant. My plan worked to perfection. After breakfast, the waitress simply rolled me to the door, where I finally managed to stand and waddle out of the restaurant about 9:00. Then I resupplied at the Exxon Mart across the road.

The AT is generally well marked in the wilderness with white blazes. However, the blazes are scarce or seemingly nonexistent when there is a major road to cross. After resupplying, I headed in the wrong direction. I followed the white reflectors on the guiderail, which looked like white blazes. After I had walked about 10 minutes, I stopped and asked some road construction workers if I was on the trail. They told me to go back in the direction I had just come and to take the road, which crossed underneath the interstate. Sure enough—I finally found a white blaze there, about a quarter mile down the road. I wondered why the trail wasn't marked more clearly so that hikers like me could make their way without confusion and outside intervention.

After lunch, I was tired and decided to stop to rest in the shade of some trees not far off the trail. I unpacked my Tyvek ground cover and took a one-hour nap. It had taken me 43 days to get my first nap on the AT. In mid-afternoon, I saw a big black snake crossing the trail in front of me. I stood in amazement as the snake crawled into a knot-hole of a downed tree just a few feet from the trail and totally disappeared. If I had arrived merely 30 seconds later, I would never have known that the snake was inside the tree.

The sky began to turn dark in the late afternoon, and rain appeared to be imminent. I stopped at 5:30 just after crossing VA 610. I had hiked 14 easy miles. I set up my tent just off the AT in a grassy area. Soon after I was in my tent, it began to rain and continued most of the night. I did not need to use the emergency sleeping bag because of the mild temperature.

Day 44—Wednesday, May 4, 2011

In the morning, it was a gloomy and damp. It was hard to get moving, and I didn't start hiking until about 8:00. Within the first 20 minutes, I found trail magic consisting of a peanut butter and jelly sandwich and soda. It tasted great! It was the only time that I experienced a ready-to-eat sandwich as trail magic. Late in the afternoon, it became windy, and the temperature dropped significantly. I climbed over 2,000 feet in four miles and reached the Chestnut Knob Shelter (4,409 ft.). After hiking more than 13 miles, I was happy to enter the shelter and get out of the elements. The shelter was formerly a fire warden's cabin and is one of just a few on the AT that is enclosed. It sleeps eight and has plexiglass windows to let in light. Within an hour, many hikers arrived. Two of those hikers headed back to the trail after a short rest. I gave no thought to resume hiking as the shelter had much more appeal. I knew many of the seven hikers who settled in for the night including Sweet Pea, Sage, Blue Eyes, and Hot Sauce.

It was a long night, a very long night. As the temperature dropped considerably, it began to hail, and the wind picked up. I put on several layers of clothes and got into my emergency sleeping bag. Within a short time there was condensation in the bag, and my clothes became damp. I was cold, miserable, and awake much of the night. It was definitely the most uncomfortable night that I spent on the AT. I kept wishing dawn would appear. I had decided before morning that the emergency sleeping bag was worthless and had to go. I decided never to use it again! I planned to dispose of it at the first opportunity and hopefully get a new sleeping bag ASAP.

Day 45—Thursday, May 5, 2011

I began hiking before 7:00 wearing my hat, jacket, and gloves. In order to generate some body heat, I tried to move quickly. By mid-morning, a pleasant day was shaping up. Soon I met a section hiker, Jerry Lehman, who I talked with extensively during the day. He gave me his phone number and offered to meet me when I got into his area near Bake Oven Knob, Pennsylvania. Little did Jerry know that I definitely planned to take him up on his offer!

Just after passing VA 615 at Laurel Creek, I saw one of the funniest things on the AT. Someone had set up a fantasy campground including a lounge chair, television, sofa, and toilet.

Fantasy campground in Virginia

It was all in good fun and likely brought a smile to every hiker that passed by. I wrote jokingly in my blog that it was where I spent most of my time on the trail. I set up camp just off the trail approximately two miles past VA 615. I had hiked nearly 17 miles. Thankfully, the temperature was warmer than the night before, so I did not use the worthless sleeping bag.

Day 46—Friday, May 6, 2011

As I started hiking at 6:30, the weather was gorgeous and the trail was not difficult. The highest elevation of the day was in mid-afternoon when I went over Bushy Mountain (3,101 ft.). Late in the afternoon, I reached VA 606 and walked a half mile down the winding road to Trent's Grocery. I bought a sandwich for dinner and a few items for resupply. As I was leaving, I disposed of my emergency sleeping bag in a trash can. It felt good to get rid of such a useless item in my back-pack. Then it was a half-mile walk back to the trail. I hiked until 7:00 before set-ting up camp just off the AT. I was pleased to have covered almost 25 miles, a new personal record. The evening temperature was mild, and I didn't miss my dis-carded sleeping bag.

Day 47—Saturday, May 7, 2011

By 6:30 in the morning, I was headed to Wood's Hole Hostel and Mountain Retreat. The first three hours of hiking were easy, before the trail became difficult and very rocky. After I had hiked about 13 miles, I came out of the woods at Sugar Run Gap Road (VA 663). I walked just a short distance down the unpaved road. The road split at that point, and there were no road signs. I pondered which way to go. I knew that the hostel was only a half mile ahead down one of the roads. But which way? I thought that perhaps the one road was really just a long drive-way. Since I could not see what was at the end, I wasn't sure. I was dismayed as I looked around for some clue as to what to do. Then I noticed a tiny, hand-writ-ten sign in a tree that pointed down the road to the hostel.

Wood's Hole Hostel and Mountain Retreat was originally an old homestead built in the 1880s. Then in 1986 Roy and Tillie Wood opened for business as a hostel. The renovated chestnut-log cabin has a covered front porch, a nearby bunkhouse, and is surrounded by the Jefferson National Forest. It is now oper-ated by the Woods' granddaughter, Neville, and her partner, Michael, who con-tinue the tradition of hosting thru-hikers.

My first task was to pick up the package containing my 30-degree sleeping bag. I also got the bounce box I had sent from Damascus. I knew before long I would be buying a lighter-weight sleeping bag and sending the warmer, bulkier bag back to Ohio.

I decided to check out the bunkhouse. After I climbed a ladder to the loft, I peered into a rather dark room. I discovered what appeared to be a vinyl-covered foam pad on the floor for sleeping, along with the gear of several hikers. It was quite warm, and the ceiling seemed to hang low. Rather than stay in the bunkhouse for $10, I elected to set up my tent in the rear of the property for $8.

Next to the bunkhouse was a solar shower. A large towel served as a shower curtain. It was quite unusual to look up and see the sky, while taking a shower. Before dinner, Neville asked everyone to introduce themselves and relate what they were most thankful for while hiking the AT. I said that I was most thankful for good health and for not needing any medication for ailments. Many hikers take Ibuprofen so often for pain that on the AT it is called the" I vitamin." The highlight of staying at the hostel was the delicious food, served family style. I enjoyed the scrumptious dinner, which cost $12.

Day 48—Sunday, May 8, 2011

It was Mother's Day, and my thoughts turned to my loving mother, Anne. She had a difficult life. When she was very young, her father left the family. Her mother had to support three daughters on her own. Because of that hardship and pain, family was the most important thing to my mother. Her greatest joy in life occurred when her family got together. When my father died suddenly while I was a sophomore in high school, my mother supported my brother and me as a single parent. She was a widow for 38 years until she died in 1998. I said a prayer for her as I reflected on all she had done for me.

Although it rained overnight, it had stopped by morning. It was not fun to pack my wet tent, but I was still satisfied with my decision not to sleep in the bunkhouse. I enjoyed a tasty and hearty breakfast, which cost $6.50. I thought of how my stay at the hostel was worthwhile because of the good food.

I looked forward to meeting friends, Dan and Vangie Gordon, about 10 miles ahead in Pearisburg. After paying my bill at the hostel, I hiked a half mile back down the unpaved road to the trail. It was exciting to think about the Gordon's offer of food and lodging. I tried to keep a good pace as I knew I didn't have much time to spare to arrive on time. While I was hiking, I was passed by a couple whom I had met at the hostel. The unusual thing was that neither of them had hiking sticks. The man had only a long pole, while the woman carried nothing for support.

I picked up my pace as I could see that I was not going to be on time to meet Dan and Vangie. In fact, I passed the couple, who had passed me earlier in the day. As I approached the road where I was to meet my friends, I hustled down several steps on an embankment. I slipped on the very last step and fell. I wasn't hurt, but my rain pants were muddy. Finally, I made it to the meeting place on North Main Street in Pearisburg at 1:15. I was thrilled to find Dan and Vangie patiently awaiting my arrival.

Before getting into Dan's truck, I took off my muddy rain pants. Fortunately, I had a pair of long pants underneath. Both my shirt and pants were wet with sweat. Dan drove me to Blacksburg to visit the campus of Virginia Tech. It traces its beginning to 1872 and has about 30,000 students on a beautiful 2,600-acre campus. Unfortunately, it was the site of the deadliest mass shootings in U.S. history. In April 2007, a disturbed student killed 32 people on campus and then shot himself. We drove by the memorial site on the campus. It made for a sad and sobering reflection of that tragic day. I thought of those killed and contemplated how fragile life can be. Certainly none of those shot and killed that morning could ever have thought of dying while simply attending or teaching a college class.

The students and athletic teams at Virginia Tech are known as Hokies. I asked Dan, who had attended Virginia Tech, "What is a hokie?" He replied, "A hokie stone is a type of limestone that is unique to Virginia and is the primary finishing material used in constructing campus buildings." In 1982 the "Hokie Bird" became the mascot of the university. The Virginia Tech Website reports the word "Hokie" was first used in the 1890s in a cheer that won first prize, now known as "Old Hokie."

After a late lunch with Dan and Vangie at O'Charley's Restaurant, I arrived at their lovely home in Christiansburg. I did my laundry, resupplied at a supermarket, enjoyed a fantastic steak dinner, related some of my trail experiences, and slept in a wonderful bed. Wow! Life could not get any better than that!

Day 49—Monday, May 9, 2011

After a five-star breakfast in the morning, which included cereal with blueberries and scrumptious French toast, I thought how fortunate I was. I felt blessed that I knew Dan and Vangie and was most thankful for their magnificent hospitality. Seeing people that I knew along the trail was truly wonderful!

About 9:30 Dan began to drive me back to the location where he and Vangie had met me the day before. I began hiking about 10:30 and soon walked along U.S. 460. I crossed the Senator Shumate Bridge looking down at the New River. Then the AT dropped down along the river. The trail appeared to continue north right along the water. I was pleased with the pretty area and flat terrain. After hiking about 10 minutes, I realized that recently I had not seen a white blaze. I walked another five minutes before I concluded that somehow I must have gotten off the trail, so back I went with a sense of anger and disgust. When I had almost gotten back to U.S. 460, I saw a white blaze leading into the woods off to the right. It was rather hidden, and I was sure that others had often missed seeing it as well.

In a short time, I thought that my pack felt extra heavy—probably because it was. I could barely get my backpack closed. In fact it wasn't really closed, since

I couldn't pull the drawstring tight. I thought how tempting the food was at the supermarket. I had fallen victim to its allure and bought too much!

In the early afternoon, I had a long climb of about 1,700 feet. I began to feel very tired and started to look for a place to rest. I found a shaded spot just off the trail. I laid out my Tyvek ground cover and napped. I heard hikers go by a few times as I slept. I even heard a hiker comment on my siesta. It was only the second nap I had taken in nearly 50 days on the trail. When I arose about an hour later, my shade had vanished. I was lying in the sun. Nevertheless, I felt refreshed as I resumed hiking.

I camped at Symms Gap Meadow (3,320 ft.) about 7:30. I had hiked about 12 miles. I had a great view in the evening of a small town along the Virginia/West Virginia border about five miles away. I went to a small pond nearby to get water. Unfortunately, the pond had scum and frogs in it, and it was most unappealing. I could not get myself to even treat the water. It was one of the few times that I turned down water, even though I was in need.

Day 50—Tuesday, May 10, 2011—Week 8

My hike began about 6:45 on a cool morning. I was eager to get to a water source before I became too dehydrated. When I found water about six miles ahead, I was glad that I had chosen not to drink the scummy pond water the night before. By mid-morning, I saw a large black snake on the trail. The snake was not eager to move until I nudged him with my hiking stick. Later I came to a fallen tree, which blocked the trail. I stepped on a branch, trying to get over it. Down I went into the mud.

In the afternoon, there was a challenging climb of over 1,000 feet. About 5:00 I reached Bailey Gap Shelter (3,525 ft.) and decided to eat dinner—a mix of mashed potatoes and salmon. I looked for several minutes in my pack for utensils, but I could not find any. Improvised methods are sometimes required on the trail, so I used my toothbrush to stir the concoction and then to eat it. Later my toothbrush served as a knife to spread peanut butter on my bagel. My toothbrush did double duty for the next few meals until I finally located my utensils. When I brushed my teeth, I delighted in the unique taste of peanut butter in my toothpaste. If Colgate ever introduces toothpaste with a peanut butter flavor, remember that I discovered it first.

After dinner, I decided to give away several food items to lessen my load so that I could properly close my backpack. Three hikers took a few items (candy and snacks) that I offered. With a slightly lighter backpack that I could now close, I was back on the AT. I hiked another three miles and set up camp just off the trail at 7:00, as rain was imminent. There were heavy thunderstorms overnight. I had hiked over 14 miles. I was disappointed that I had failed to get water at the shelter, but I had chosen not to because I was nearly out of Aqua Mira, my water treatment.

Day 51—Wednesday, May 11, 2011

By 6:45 in the morning, I was back hiking, eager once again to find a water source as I was completely out. I really wanted to find a spring, so the water would not need to be treated. After hiking about five miles, I said a prayer, asking God to guide me to a spring. Within 10 seconds after I concluded my prayer, I was astonished as I saw a spring a few feet off the trail. There was a flow of cold water coming right out of a rock. My prayer was heard, and I marveled at how quickly God had responded to my request. I drank a large amount of water, thinking how good it tasted, before filling my Camelbak.

The AT was more difficult than it had been recently. There were ascents totaling 2,200 feet and descents totaling more than 3,200 feet. On one of the descents, I fell on a wet rock. Once again, I was not hurt. As I thought about the fall, I concluded that I should completely avoid slippery mud, tree branches, tree roots, and wet rocks. At the rate I was going, I thought how the trail offered really no safe places of passage. In the afternoon, I was pleased to find trail magic. A cold soda and cookies really hit the spot. Bless that trail angel who brightened my day and gave me new energy!

In the early evening, I passed by Keffer Oak, the largest oak tree on the AT in the south. It is estimated to be 300 years old. When it was last measured several years ago, its girth was over 18 feet. As evening settled in, I began to look for a campsite. Usually in the southern states there are many spots to camp. I passed by Sarver Hollow Shelter (3,000 ft.) because it was .3 of a mile off the AT. As I kept moving ahead, the terrain became more rocky and uneven.

It was getting dark about 8:00, and rain began to fall lightly. I had hiked more than 18 miles. I had been looking for a place for a while to set up camp. Since I could not find a level spot, I decided reluctantly to set up my tent on the edge of the rather narrow trail. Although I was partially blocking the trail, I felt that I had no other choice. It was the only time I ever did that. I was concerned with the unlikely event of a hiker coming along the trail in darkness and tripping over my tent.

Day 52—Thursday, May 12, 2011

It was a damp day as I began hiking again at 6:45. I was pleased that my tent did not seem to cause a problem for any hiker. However, I pledged not to wait so long again in the evening to begin looking for a campsite. At Sinking Creek Mountain (3,450 ft.), the AT crosses a significant "continental divide." The side of the ridge the water flows down determines whether it drains eventually into the Gulf of Mexico (west side) or the Atlantic Ocean (east side).

I was fortunate to find a spring in the late morning, which meant I didn't need to treat the water. It was cloudy and foggy all day. When I stopped for a break in the late morning, a hiker I had met several days previously named Rain

Gear caught up with me. He had slept in the Sarver Hollow Shelter the night before. I had avoided that shelter because it was .3 of a mile off the AT. There were no other hikers in the shelter with Rain Gear, but there were mice. In fact, a mouse got into his hair twice during the night. My longest climb was about 1,600 feet, but there were steep descents of 1,600 feet and nearly 2,000 feet.

I decided to visit the Audie Murphy Monument located on a blue-blazed trail on Brushy Mountain. Murphy was the most decorated American soldier of World War II. He died at age 46 in a plane crash near the site of the monument in May 1971. The granite monument was decorated with American flags and some flowers. I was thrilled that I had seen it and paid tribute to a truly great American hero.

A light rain and thunder started about 3:30. After hiking about 16 miles, I stopped at the Pickle Branch Shelter at 5:00. The only other person at the shelter was a hiker that I met for the first time named Gotta Go. I asked him if on the following day he would want to go to Trail Days, an annual festival for hikers in Damascus, Virginia. He declined the offer. When it was almost dark, I decided to set up my tent inside the shelter as there was plenty of space. The shelter slept six people and only Gotta Go and I were there. While I slept in my tent under the roof of the shelter, I was protected against rain, mosquitoes, and mice. I went to sleep soon after supper, anticipating an early start the next day.

Day 53—Friday, May 13, 2011

When I awoke in the morning, I was surprised to find that three more hikers had arrived at the shelter after I had gone to sleep. Since I didn't take up a huge amount of space with my tent, there was still adequate room for the three hikers. After a good night's sleep, I eagerly began hiking by 6:00. I needed to walk over 12 miles to reach the Catawba Valley General Store by 2:00 to get a prearranged ride to Trail Days.

Trail Days has the atmosphere of a festival. It is an annual event that was first held in Damascus in May 1987 to commemorate the 50th anniversary of the opening of the AT in 1937. Although Trail Days lasts one week, the main activities are on the weekend. It offers hikers a chance to meet friends, take in hiking-related exhibits and presentations, and participate in a parade.

In the morning, I saw a box tortoise on the trail for the third time. I thought of the story of the "Tortoise and the Hare." In a similar manner, I was akin to the hare as I hiked along at a much faster pace than any tortoise. I wondered if there was really only one tortoise that perhaps I had seen three times. While I slept each night, it may have kept on truckin'. If that were the case, it was doing a great job of keeping up with me, even though it moved at a much slower pace.

In about four miles, I reached Cove Mountain (3,020 ft.). It is an area that I knew was difficult with extremely rocky, steep, and rugged terrain. Furthermore,

I was hiking over it on of all days—Friday the thirteenth! I consider Cove Mountain to be the most dangerous spot of the AT. A misstep there on the ledge would most likely have been my last. The trail was only inches wide with a deep drop-off.

Dangerous trail on Cove Mountain, VA

Fortunately, I met Gotta Go on Cove Mountain near a formation called Dragons Tooth. He had left the shelter before me in the morning. I caught up with him only because he had become confused about the location of the trail. When I met him, he was very unhappy. He had hiked a long way down a steep pile of rocks. Eventually, he realized that he had not seen a white blaze for a while, so he had to climb back up the jagged pile of rocks a good distance to the trail. That's where I happened to meet him.

As we were descending over 1,000 feet down the mountain, we talked about how the trail was not well marked in some spots and how frustrating it can become.

After he calmed down from his annoying ordeal, I again offered him a ride to Trail Days for the weekend. He briefly reconsidered and accepted. When Gotta Go and I reached the parking lot on VA 311, we had hiked over 12 miles. There we met two other aspiring thru-hikers (Moses and Pele), who were looking for a ride to Trail Days. I told them that I knew someone who would provide a ride for them. We walked a mile down the road to the Catawba Valley General Store, arriving at 1:45. We bought a soda and a snack before our ride arrived.

I had arranged to meet Lil' Bit (Wendy Palmer) at 2:00 at the Post Office, which was directly across the street from the store. I had first met her in Florida shortly before the start of my hike through Paul Landrigan, a friend of my cousin, Patty Mattson. Lil' Bit had offered to give me and three other hikers of my choice a ride to Trail Days. When she thru-hiked the AT in 2004, she had gotten a ride to Trail Days. She said that it was a fun event, and I needed to go.

Lil' Bit had quite a compelling story. A female friend suggested that together they hike the trail in 2004. Lil' Bit's husband agreed to take care of their two children while she took a six-month hike. Once on the trail, she broke her ankle in Virginia, tripped while crossing a bridge in NY breaking her nose, and suffered Lyme disease in New England, yet she completed the thru-hike. I was so impressed by her determination and courage. I called Lil Bit a warrior. I can't imagine how she had the will to keep going while coping with such medical problems.

TRAIL DAYS

Lil' Bit arrived just after 2:00. Because all of our gear didn't fit into the back of her vehicle, we had to tie down a few backpacks on the roof. It took a few hours of driving to reach Damascus. At Trail Days, most hikers camp at the edge of town on Shady Lane, where there is a large grassy area. In addition, camping is allowed in the nearby wooded area, where rowdy hikers tend to congregate. I set up my tent on the grassy expanse.

Vendors set up booths in the nearby parking lot to promote hiking-related equipment. In the evening, I got in line for free food provided by a company. It consisted of a bowl of chili, a piece of bread and a few cookies. One hiker complained that the amount of food did not exactly make a full-course meal. I agreed, but I thought of the saying, "Beggars can't be choosers." It began to rain late Friday afternoon and continued intermittently all weekend. Several hikers told me that it often rained at Trail Days.

Day 54—Saturday, May 14, 2011

I looked forward to only my fourth zero day after having completed nearly 700 miles on the AT. Before 8:00 in the morning, I hitched a short ride to the public bathroom in town to take a shower. While I was getting dressed after showering, a man (Ken Mauck) entered. After we talked for several minutes, he offered me a ride to breakfast at a local restaurant. I was very happy to accept! After breakfast, I went to Mount Rogers Outfitters and bought a down-filled sleeping bag rated at 45 degrees to replace my 30-degree bag. Finally, I had a smaller and lighter-weight sleeping bag that I could use the rest of the hike! I also bought more Aqua Mira to treat ground water.

Outside the store was a man, Gene Espy, who was standing next to a table containing a stack of paperback books for sale. I decided to buy his book, *The Trail of My Life: The Gene Espy Story*. In 1951, Gene became only the second person to successfully thru-hike the AT at age 24. Earl Shaffer, now deceased, was the first to thru-hike the trail in 1948 at the age of 30. It was a thrill to meet and talk with Gene, a humble and kind 84-year-old man. Exactly 60 years ago, Gene had dealt with many of the same hardships and joys that I was experiencing. I wondered if someday a relative of mine might hike the trail, perhaps many decades in the future. That thought brought a smile to my face.

My next stop was at the Post Office, where I shipped home my 30-degree sleeping bag for the second time. I had sent it home first from Damascus before it was returned to me at Wood's Hole Hostel. Now I was sending it back home again. This time it would stay home for good! If that bag could talk, it would probably say it had traveled more miles since late April via the U.S. Postal Service than I had on the AT since March. At the same time, I remembered the deplorable emergency sleeping bag that had caused me so much distress!

I also sent home a pair of gloves and two long-sleeved shirts. I reasoned that summer-like weather was just around the corner. Just as I was about to leave the Post Office, Swamp Dawg came in. He seemed happy and was hiking with several others on the trail. His average hike was 10 miles per day. Just prior to Trail Days, he had been in Atkins, Virginia. I was exactly 160 miles ahead of him on the AT. I expected our meeting to be the last time I would see him during my hike.

At 2:00 I went to the popular parade through downtown. The annual event brought out all the "crazies" in full force. Hikers were grouped by the year they hiked the trail. Some hikers wore silly hats, and many carried water balloons. Many spectators carried large squirt guns or water soakers, which were intended to nearly drown their victims.

Day 55—Sunday, May 15, 2011

It rained fairly hard overnight, but the carousers were not to be denied. Sometime in the wee hours, sleeping hikers were startled by the noise of loud drums as revelers walked through the camping area. In the morning, I was at the sink in the restroom when a man next to me complained about his sore hands, which looked raw. He said that he had gotten carried away the night before and beat his drum for many hours. He had caused me and nearly everyone else to be awakened out of a sound sleep. I thought how too much alcohol can contribute to some wild and crazy behavior!

Lil' Bit had said she would drive us back to the trail on Sunday morning. Instead, she arranged a ride for us. Two former hikers who were driving home to Pennsylvania agreed to take us. Unfortunately, the new driver was hung over from partying on Saturday evening. We didn't leave until after he was up and alert, which was well into the afternoon. Driving north of Damascus we viewed the devastation caused by the recent tornado, which hammered the area less than three weeks before. Roofs of many buildings were gone, and some businesses were leveled. I recalled that several people had died from the deadly tornado.

We reached the trailhead of the AT at the parking lot on VA 311 at 5:30. Then Gotta Go and I hiked about four miles to McAfee Knob (3,197 ft.). It is considered by many to provide the best view in Virginia. I would agree completely. A high rock juts out over a pretty valley thousands of feet below, giving a spectacular panoramic view of homes and farms.

McAfee Knob—"the best view in VA"

Some hikers sit on the edge of the rock with their feet dangling, but I didn't feel that brave. I went near the edge and surveyed the great vista. That was close enough for me.

There is no camping at McAfee Knob, so Gotta Go and I resumed hiking. In about a half mile, we reached the Campbell Shelter (2,580 ft.) at 8:15. We had completed less than five miles in our abbreviated day of hiking. When it was almost dark, I set up my tent in the shelter as we were the only hikers there.

Day 56—Monday, May 16, 2011

Gotta Go was leaving in the morning, just about the time I was getting up. Before he headed down the trail, I wished him well and said good bye. He carried an extremely light backpack. Since he was a young, strong, and fast hiker, I expected to never see him again, and my expectation was correct. Soon after I began hiking at 7:30, I fell on a large piece of tree bark that covered the trail. It felt as if I had stepped on a banana peel. I wasn't hurt, and the worst thing was that I had some mud on my pant leg. I laughed as I thought that tree bark was another thing to add to my list of things to avoid stepping on.

After I hiked about five miles, I reached a half-mile stretch known as Tinker Cliffs (3,000 ft.). I appreciated the great vistas, as I stopped several times to look back toward McAfee Knob. Tinker Cliffs is said to have derived its name from Revolutionary War deserters. These men repaired pots and pans and were known as tinkers.

I felt fatigued after lunch, so I found a shaded spot just off the trail. I put down my Tyvek ground cover, wadded up my jacket as a pillow, and took a nap for an hour. When I awoke, I felt strong, refreshed, and ready to conquer the trail. For most of the remaining afternoon, I was descending. After hiking over 15 miles, I reached U.S. 220 at Daleville about 5:00. A Pizza Hut was just a hundred feet away. I quickly decided that I could not pass by without having dinner, so I stopped, ordered a pizza, and enjoyed the AYCE salad bar.

As I left the restaurant about 6:00, I planned to resume my hike, but I immediately had a change of heart. The sky looked threatening, and I spotted a Howard Johnson Express Inn directly across the street. The Inn offered a single rate of $40, including a hot breakfast. I decided to take advantage of the opportunity to shower, charge my phone and camera, dry out my gear, sleep in a bed, watch television, and have a hot breakfast.

Day 57—Tuesday, May 17, 2011—Week 9

After breakfast, I enjoyed reading the newspaper and making a few phone calls. I didn't begin hiking until 9:40, which was one of my later starts on the trail. There was one steep ascent of over 1,200 feet in the morning. The great breakfast served as a real energy boost, and I hiked until mid-afternoon before eating lunch at the Wilson Creek Shelter (1,830 ft.), which was well into Central Virginia.

After hiking about 14 miles with rain falling lightly, I reached Black House Gap (2,402 ft.), the southernmost point where the AT meets the Blue Ridge Parkway. At that point the AT runs nearly parallel with the Blue Ridge Parkway and then the Skyline Drive for almost 200 miles. When the Blue Ridge Parkway was built, it displaced the original AT and required a major relocation of the trail. During the next few miles, I crossed the Parkway four times.

I expected to stay at the Bobblets Gap Shelter (1,920 ft.), which was .2 of a mile off the trail. When I arrived there, I was disappointed to find the shelter full and the few decent campsites taken. In fact there were several campers who had set up their tents on uneven ground. I knew better than that. Although it was soon to be dark, I had no choice but to keep hiking. After securing water from a spring near the shelter, I hiked back to the trail and resumed heading north.

With each step I took, I surveyed the land for a good location to set up my tent. In about a half mile, I spotted a small but level patch of ground about 10 yards off the trail. However, before I could even remove my backpack, it began to rain much harder. I knew that if I attempted to set up my tent, all my things would get wet, so I simply stood by the site and said a prayer for the rain to let up for just ten minutes. I knew from experience that it took me about ten minutes to set up my tent and get all my gear inside. Within several minutes, my prayers were answered as the rain lessened to little more than a mist. It was slightly after 8:00, and I was very pleased to have hiked almost 19 miles.

Day 58—Wednesday, May 18, 2011

The rain had stopped in the morning, and I began hiking about 8:15. I crossed the Blue Ridge Parkway three times within two hours. I was delighted to find trail magic at VA 43, Bearwallow Gap. It was quite surprising that it included snack crackers, zucchini bread, Frosted Mini-Wheats, and soda. Zucchini bread and cereal were never offered as trail magic anywhere else on the AT. I had planned to get off the trail six miles ahead at VA 614, Jennings Creek, and hitch a ride a few miles to resupply. After finding the trail magic, I decided to change my plan.

After lunch at the Bryant Ridge Shelter (1,320 ft.), I climbed over 2,200 feet to reach Floyd Mountain (3,560 ft.). The day was quite pleasant until late in the afternoon when it began to rain. After I passed the Cornelius Creek Shelter (3,145 ft.), I saw a flat area with acres of rhododendron bushes. I veered off the trail and walked into the thicket of bushes, wandering around looking for an area large enough to set up my tent. It was more difficult than I had expected. Finally, I located a satisfactory spot well off the trail. I had hiked more than 18 miles.

Day 59—Thursday, May 19, 2011

Before I began to hike in the morning, I had an unexpected problem. After I took down my tent and packed my gear, I surveyed the area. All I could see were rhododendron bushes in all directions. I had no idea where the trail was. I knew I couldn't be more than .1 of a mile from it. But which way? I walked one way for a few minutes with no luck. I turned and walked in another direction for a few minutes. Then I turned yet again and walked a while, and still I saw no sign of the trail. I stopped and felt a sick feeling from walking in circles.

Then I became excited when I noticed a hiker walking perhaps 75 yards away. I didn't think he saw me. I recognized the hiker as a man that I had passed on the trail late the prior afternoon. I headed in his direction and caught up with him within a few minutes. I said," Good morning and thank you!" He look at me puzzled and replied, "Good morning, but what are you thanking me for?" I explained, "I camped overnight in the thicket of rhododendron bushes and became confused this morning where the trail was. Then I saw you as you passed by." He just smiled at my comment. He had no idea of the real appreciation I had for his unintended help. I believe that my confusion probably cost me about 10 minutes of wasted time. However, without the hiker's help, it could have been much longer!

As the morning unfolded, I climbed Apple Orchard Mountain (4225 ft.), the highest point on the trail until New Hampshire. A moment later, the trail passed directly under a rock formation called "the guillotine." The name is derived from a good-sized boulder that is cradled precariously above and between two larger boulders. It appears that the stone might be in danger of falling and smashing anyone who happened to be hiking underneath it. In reality, the guillotine has been in the same position for a very long time.

About noon, I stopped for lunch at the Thunder Hill Shelter (3,960 ft.). Just as I was arriving, Rain Gear was leaving. He said that his dad was meeting him about 5:30 at the James River Foot Bridge, where the AT meets VA 501. He was going home to Lynchburg, Virginia for the weekend. Then Rain Gear made me a great offer. If I would be at the bridge by 5:30, his dad would be willing to drive me six miles to Glasgow, Virginia, to resupply and then drive me back to the trail. That was a fantastic offer, but it caused a major concern for me. I was about 14 miles from the bridge, and I would need to hike at a fast pace for about six hours to get there on time.

I decided to try to take advantage of Rain Gear's offer. I quickly ate lunch and resumed hiking. The weather was good, and the terrain was fairly easy with only moderate climbs and mostly well-graded descents. Even as I got tired, I felt motivated to keep hiking. I crossed the Blue Ridge Parkway three times in the afternoon. When I was on reasonably flat ground, I tried to quicken my pace. I

Walking under "the guillotine" in VA

did not take a break for four hours. Just two miles from the bridge, the trail passed directly in front of the Matts Creek Shelter (835 ft.). I was surprised to see Rain Gear there talking with several other hikers. I knew then that my goal for the afternoon was going to be met. After I crossed the 625-foot bridge, I met Rain Gear's father who drove me and three other hikers to resupply. Upon our return, I resumed hiking. At 8:00 I camped just before the Johns Hollow Shelter (1,020 ft.). I basked in the satisfaction of having resupplied and having hiked over 22 miles.

Day 60—Friday, May 20, 2011

In the morning, I climbed over 2,300 feet to scale Bluff Mountain (3,372 ft.). I stopped at the Punch Bowl Shelter (2,500 ft.) for lunch. I had planned to get water there, but the source was a scummy pond. I elected to pass on the pond water. As I was finishing lunch, two hikers (Leap and Spot) arrived. I had spoken with Leap on several previous occasions, but I had never met Spot. Leap was a likeable young man from Iowa, and he was thoroughly enjoying his adventure. He had quit his job right before starting his hike and hoped to make a career involving some aspect of hiking.

When I met Spot, his name reminded me of a pet dog. His trail name was derived from the beginning of his last name, which sounded very Italian to me. He said that his friends had always called him Spot. He had worked in various construction trades and had quit his most recent job. After he returned from his current hike, he was quite confident he could find employment with his diverse trade skills. This was his sixth attempt to thru-hike the AT. Yes, the sixth time! He was successful three times, while on two occasions he was not. One hike ended abruptly because his daughter became quite ill. The other aborted attempt happened when he stepped off a high curb in Harpers Ferry, West Virginia, badly spraining his ankle. I tried to grasp the thought of me thru-hiking the AT more than once. That thought would just not compute!

Immediately after finishing my lunch, I resumed hiking alone. After going 15 miles, I decided to set up camp in the evening at a small campsite just a few feet off the trail. As I was setting up my tent, Leap and Spot approached. Leap continued hiking, while Spot decided to call it a day. He selected a site within 30 feet of mine on the other side of the trail. We conversed as we made camp and ate supper. I peppered him with questions about his hiking experiences. I was fascinated by a claim that Spot made. He said, "Although I am not a fast hiker, I usually hike 25-30 miles per day." How could that be? I questioned his claim, "You usually hike 25-30 miles per day?" He replied, "The reason I am able to hike that far on most days is because I begin hiking very early in the morning and quit usually later in the evening." I was much impressed with Spot's apparent discipline, determination, and stamina.

Day 61—Saturday, May 21, 2011

I awoke soon after daybreak. I was startled to see that Spot was already putting on his backpack to begin hiking. A moment later, he was on the trail and out of sight. It was the last time I saw him. After he was gone, I reflected on his statement the night before that he was an early riser. So was I, but I felt that Spot was perhaps in a league above me. Spot's fast start made me want to start hiking as quickly as possible. For one of the few times on the trail, I decided to forego breakfast. I was on the trail within a half hour. In about three miles, I reached the Brown Mountain Creek Shelter (1,395 ft.). I decided to cook oatmeal, which I had found in a hiker box some time ago.

At lunch time, I reached the Cow Camp Gap Shelter (3,160 ft.). I noticed birds nesting in the outside corner of the shelter and took a picture of what appeared to be the mother and three babies. After I left the shelter, I climbed Cold Mountain (4,022 ft.). About a half hour later, I saw a big groundhog as it crossed the dirt road at Hog Camp Gap (3,485 ft.). It was 20 feet away, and I stared at it for several seconds. As I reached for my camera, it went the other way. When it was about 100 feet away, it stopped, turned, and stared at me for a few seconds before continuing on its way.

In early evening, I stopped to eat supper. As I was eating, I realized I was nearly out of water. I did not stop for water several miles earlier because the water source was downhill and quite a distance off the trail. As I was preparing to leave and head north, a southbound day hiker approached. His name was Jerry Nichols, and he was from West Virginia. I summoned the courage to ask him, "Do you have any water you could spare?" He replied, "Well, I don't need the liter and a half of water I am carrying because I am almost back to my car, which is parked at the next road." Then he reached into his pack and said, "You can have this bottle of Gatorade as well." I was amazed by my good fortune! I felt like I had just won the lottery. It was another example of trail magic. It felt like divine intervention— God was helping me out through Jerry's kindness.

Because I had plenty of fluids thanks to Jerry, I felt relieved as I hiked until 8:15. After hiking nearly eighteen miles, I set up my tent at a campsite just before dark at the North Fork of the Piney River. There were no other hikers at the campsite. Since I wanted to stay at the Dutch Haus B & B in Montebello, Virginia, the following day, I called to make a reservation. I asked the owner, Lois Arnold, if there was a church service that I could attend in the immediate area. Lois told me that if I arrived in time to attend an 11:00 service, she would arrange for me to get a ride from a family who lived nearby.

Day 62—Sunday, May 22, 2011

I was awake very early in the morning. Getting to the Dutch Haus B & B required hiking nearly a mile off the trail down a steep road. I arrived at the Dutch Haus in plenty of time to shower and do laundry. About 10:45, a couple (Betty & Lester Roberts) arrived and drove me to church. After the service, the couple's two grandchildren (Nathan and LeeAnn) rode with us back to the Dutch Haus. I asked Nathan, "How old are you?" He raised three fingers and said, "I'm three!" I was highly amused by his sister's quick matter-of-fact comment, "I'm six, and it takes _two_ of him to make _one_ of me."

The Dutch Haus advertises a free lunch to all thru-hikers, whether or not they stay there. The offer is a kind gesture to help aspiring thru-hikers. Furthermore, some hikers who stop for a free lunch end up staying overnight. At lunch time, a thru-hiker (Peregrine) identified the birds in the photo I had taken the day before at a shelter as Phoebe Fly Catchers.

Day 63—Monday, May 23, 2011

My stay at the Dutch Haus was quite enjoyable. After a hearty breakfast, I trudged uphill on the rocky road almost a mile to get back to the trail. In the late morning, I crossed a mountain called The Priest (4,063 feet), the highest elevation point of the day. Then over the next four miles, I descended about 3,100 feet to VA 56, Tye River (970 ft.). Finally, I began my last ascent of over 2,200 feet to Chimney Rocks (3,190 ft.), where I discovered a great one-person campsite next to a boulder. I had hiked over 14 miles.

Day 64—Tuesday, May 24, 2011—Week 10

I began to hike at 7:00 on an empty stomach. Over the first four miles, I had a 700-foot climb followed by a descent of over 1,100-feet before reaching the Maupin Field Shelter (2,720 ft.). I was hungry, so I boiled water to prepare oatmeal. Even though I thoroughly enjoyed the oatmeal, it was the last time I cooked it because of the messy cleanup.

When I crossed the Blue Ridge Parkway for the final time, I stopped to eat lunch. I sat on the curb of the Dipping Rock Parking Area. I decided to cook, which was very unusual for lunch. After getting over Humpback Mountain (3,250 ft.) in the late afternoon, the rest of the day was relatively easy. When I reached the Paul Wolfe Shelter (1,700 ft.) about 8:00, I had completed 20 miles in a 13-hour day of hiking. I set up my tent and had a quick supper of cheese on a bagel as darkness arrived.

Day 65—Wednesday, May 25, 2011

I had only a five-mile hike to reach the road heading into Waynesboro. I took my time in the morning as I left at 8:45 on the well-worn path, directly in front of the shelter. It was the same path that another hiker had taken about 45 minutes earlier. After hiking 10 minutes, I realized that I had not seen any white blazes. I turned around and headed back toward the shelter. I was upset with my situation. How could I have gotten off the trail again? When I got to the shelter, a close examination revealed the problem. Just after passing the shelter, the trail turned immediately to the left, although the well-worn path continued straight ahead. I thought that that the path around the shelter was simply a trail leading to water or the privy, as it often does. However, there was a white blaze about 30 yards down the path, which could not be seen easily from the shelter. Although I was unhappy, I felt less self-critical. I was sure that many hikers, including the one who had left ahead of me, had made the same mistake.

After I had hiked several miles, I saw two hikers, Sage and Sweet Pea, standing on the trail ahead of me drinking sodas. There was trail magic again! After we all had finished our beverages, we hiked a short distance to reach U.S. 250. Sage and I sat by the side of the road while Sweet Pea hitched a ride for us. Sage had hiked for some time with Sweet Pea and said an advantage of hiking with a female was that it was easier to hitch a ride! Within five minutes, a man stopped. He drove us into Waynesboro to Ming Garden, a Chinese restaurant offering an

AYCE lunch buffet for only $7.15. The lunch featured great food, including apple pie ala mode for dessert. It was a real bargain for hungry hikers.

After lunch, I walked across the street to the Salvation Army store. Since my weight had dropped considerably, I needed a belt to keep my pants up. I found one to fit me that was priced at $1.00. However, it was Wednesday, which was half-price day. What a find! So for the grand total of 50 cents, I met a personal need while possibly protecting others from my indecent exposure!

Next, I walked to the YMCA and took a shower. A local trail angel covered the cost of a shower for any thru-hiker. Feeling clean and refreshed, I went to the library and used the internet. Finally, I headed nearby to the Grace Evangelical Lutheran Church Hostel. On Wednesday evenings in hiking season, the church offers a free dinner to thru-hikers. It was just luck on my part that I arrived in Waynesboro on Wednesday. The buffet featured a lot of great food including dessert. I was so full after dinner that I thought of returning the belt I had just bought as I was sure I would not need it.

After dinner, I walked to a laundromat. On my way back, I resupplied at a supermarket, where I bought a half-gallon of chocolate milk. After I had drunk a quart, I was full. However, I didn't want to throw away the rest, so I drank it. I felt bloated and regretted my gluttony for several hours.

I went to sleep on my air mattress on the floor in the church basement along-side a host of other hikers. Soon I was awakened by snoring, so I got up and moved to the music room, where I was alone. I should have taken my air mattress with me to sleep on. Instead, I pushed together three cushion chairs and slept on them, but it didn't make for a restful night's sleep.

Day 66— Thursday, May 26, 2011

I was up the next morning at 5:30 to pack, eat breakfast, and get an early ride to the trail. I was impressed by the long list of Waynesboro residents who offered to drive hikers to and from the trail. A volunteer drove another hiker and me back to the trail at 7:00 and dropped us off at Rockfish Gap. Although Damascus claims to be the friendliest town on the trail, I believe that title could just as well belong to Waynesboro.

SHENANDOAH NATIONAL PARK (SNP)

It was a short walk of less than a mile down the trail to the entrance of Shenandoah National Park (SNP), where I stopped and filled out the permit form at a kiosk. Thru-hikers entering the park via the AT are not charged a fee. The AT traverses 103 miles of a well-graded trail in SNP, which has many memorable vistas and abundant wildlife. I looked forward to hiking there because I knew it was one of the more picturesque places on the trail.

There were no extensive changes in elevation, but there were many 300-500 foot climbs and descents. I needed to rest twice during the day because of the poor sleep I had at the church hostel. During the day, I crossed Skyline Drive nine times.

After hiking about 20 miles, I arrived at the Blackrock Hut (2,645 ft.) at 7:15 and set up my tent. In SNP, a permanent structure for an overnight stay is called a hut, rather than a shelter. That evening there was a notice posted inside the hut announcing a free picnic supper for thru-hikers the following day. That news was music to my ears. The picnic location was about 20 miles ahead, where the AT crossed Skyline Drive at Smith Roach Gap.

Day 67—Friday, May 27, 2011

The start of Memorial Day weekend was clear, cool, and ideal for hiking. It was also an easy day with relatively moderate changes in elevation. I met two section hikers on the trail in the morning. They told me that there was trail magic at campsite # C-55 of the Loft Mountain Campground (3,300 ft.). After hiking over seven miles, I made it to the entrance of the campground and got a map. In about 10 minutes, I found the campsite. Three other hikers that I knew were there sitting in lawn chairs. They were talking with the man who was providing the trail magic. He had hiked the trail and had worked on its upkeep as a member of the Potomac AT Club. The club is one of 31 that put in countless hours in trail maintenance, so that the hikers like me can enjoy it. The conversation among the hikers, along with a cold soda and a bag of chips, made the 15-minute respite worthwhile. As I headed back to the trail, I first stopped at the Loft Mountain Wayside to buy a few snacks and a pint of chocolate milk. After drinking a half gallon of chocolate milk in Waynesboro in one night, I realized that a pint was sufficient.

About 4:30, I reached the picnic site at Smith Roach Gap. I discovered about a dozen hikers mingling, eating, and enjoying a feast. The food was good and plentiful, and a real delight for sure! The sponsors of the picnic were a married couple. The woman had thru-hiked the AT twice, while her husband had hiked sections of the trail. The picnic had become an annual event for them on Friday of the Memorial Day Weekend. As the picnic was winding down, the sky began to darken, and the possibility of a rain storm became evident.

I resumed hiking, and in just over a mile, I reached the Hightop Hut (3,175 ft.). I quickly found a good spot to set up my tent. I decided to get water and headed to a piped spring not far from the shelter. The water was cold and delicious. I drank some on site and quickly filled by Camelbak. I headed back to my tent hurriedly, as the rain clouds and increasing wind were warning of a storm very soon. After I was in my tent a few minutes, the rain came. As I reviewed the day, I realized that I hiked over 21 miles and had crossed Skyline Drive ten times, one more than the previous day. I was blessed to enjoy a fine day of hiking, generous hospitality, great food, and the comfort and protection from rain that my tent offered. Life was indeed good!

Day 68—Saturday, May 28, 2011

By morning, the rain had ceased, but it was much cooler than the day before. I packed my wet tent and began hiking at 6:45. After I had hiked about 12 miles, I stopped at the Lewis Mountain Campground (3,500 ft.). I bought a soda at the camp store, sat on the front porch, and ate lunch with several other hikers.

When I finished eating, I headed back toward the trail, but first I stopped and talked with two hikers who were setting up their tents to spend the night. I was feeling a little sleepy after lunch and was tempted to call it a day. Since it was only mid-afternoon, I decided to resume hiking. In about five miles I reached Hazeltop Mountain (3,812 ft.), the highest elevation of the day. I continued on toward the Big Meadows Wayside/Grill where I expected to eat dinner and resupply.

By early evening, I reached the Big Meadows Campground. I eventually saw what looked like the last campsite before the trail turned and reentered the woods. I walked about 30 yards down a path to where people were milling around a picnic table. As I neared the campsite, I said, "Could you tell me the direction to the Wayside/Grill?" A man nearest me replied, "Well, it's back about a mile in the direction you just came." That wasn't what I wanted to hear. I wasn't about to retrace my steps that far. Then the man asked me, "Would you like some water?" I quickly replied, "Thank you! That would be great." I walked with him toward the picnic table and billowing smoke from a grill. He introduced himself as Jim Lilly.

I sat down at the picnic table talking with Jim and his daughter. They had just recently completed hiking a nearby section of the AT and planned to complete the entire trail over the next several years. After a few minutes, Jim's wife asked me if I would like something to eat. Soon, I was eating steak, grilled onions, bread, and an apple. After about a half hour, I thanked the Lilly family for their hospitality and resumed hiking. I thought of how my misfortune of not seeing signage for the Wayside/Grill had brought me trail magic. In about a mile, I crossed Skyline Drive for the sixth and final time of the day. About two miles later, I was almost to the Rock Spring Hut (3,465 ft.) when I decided that darkness no longer made it safe to keep hiking. I set up my tent just off the trail, having hiked nearly 24 miles.

Day 69—Sunday, May 29, 2011

I began hiking on an empty stomach at 7:00 as I was determined to eat breakfast or brunch at the Skyland Dining Room. After a hike of a little less than five miles, I reached the Skyland Service Road, which led .2 of a mile to the restaurant. I was pleased to take advantage of a delicious buffet. In the early afternoon, I saw something quite large moving behind the trees and brush about 30 yards from the trail. I stopped, expecting to see my first bear, but it was just a deer. That wasn't too exciting as I had seen hundreds of deer near my home in the Cleveland Metro Park.

In the late afternoon, my toes hurt badly on a long descent over a very rocky, rugged, and steep trail. I went from Mary's Mountain (3,514 ft.) to Thornton Gap (2,307 ft.) in a little less than two miles. As my foot moved forward and downward on the descent, my toes were pressed hard into the front of my boot. Each step caused me to grimace. It was the worst my toes hurt on the entire hike. When I reached Thornton Gap, I stopped and took off my socks and boots. I put moleskin over several of my toes. As I resumed hiking, I definitely felt some needed relief.

After the first few weeks of hiking, I had mistakenly thought that my feet would not be much of a problem. However, I had completed nearly ten weeks of my long-distance hike, and I expected my feet to toughen. When one of my toes suffered severe trauma, the nail began to turn black. Over time the pain diminished, and a new toenail began to emerge. During the entire hike, I had four new toenails.

I was able to hike another six miles. I found a flat campsite on a side trail, about a hundred yards off the AT. After hiking over 19 miles, I began to set up my tent at 6:30. Unfortunately, it was only about 50 yards from Skyline Drive. The trees around my tent only partially obscured me from being seen from the road. That made me nervous as the ATC advises not to camp near a road for security reasons. As I was putting up my tent, I noticed something moving about 25 feet away. Once again, it was just a deer, which slowly wandered away. Just a few minutes later after I got into my tent, I saw a wild turkey 20 feet directly in front of my entrance. The turkey kept looking at the ground, trying to find morsels of food. When it was dark a few hours later, I felt relieved as my tent could not be seen from the road.

Day 70—Monday, May 30, 2011

I began hiking before breakfast on Memorial Day. I planned to eat at Elkwallow Wayside/Grill, which was just off the trail about three miles ahead. I arrived there about 8:20 and was disappointed to find that the restaurant didn't open until 9:00. After breakfast, I bought a few food items and resumed hiking. The rocky trail continued to be tough on my feet. After hiking almost 950 miles since late March, I was excited to see a black bear after crossing Skyline Drive at Rattlesnake Point Overlook. It was about 100 feet away and didn't seem to even notice me.

A black bear in Shenandoah National Park

As I walked along the trail in the noonday sun, I was getting thirsty. At that point the trail was running about 20 yards below Skyline Drive. I looked up to a small parking area just off the roadway and saw people standing around a van. I said, "Hello, do you have anything cold to drink?" It's hard for me to believe I was that bold. I can't imagine doing that now! The people looked down at me in disbelief. From where they were standing, they could not even see the trail. I'm sure they thought that I was a vagrant, wandering in the wilderness. They may have thought that I was deranged. After all, who yells out to strangers, asking if they have anything cold to drink? After a significant pause, a kind voice asked, "Would you like a bottle of Gatorade?" I responded, "That would be great!" I began to climb and fight my way through the dense underbrush up to the level of Skyline Drive.

The cold drink was just what I needed on a warm day. My benefactors were members of the Makowski family. They were not familiar at all with the AT. They were on their way to the Elkwallow Wayside/Grill, where I had eaten breakfast.

After several minutes of conversation about my adventure, Mike Makowski asked me if he could take a photo of me. I was pleased to add Mike to my list of people who could follow my AT progress on my blog. The rest of the warm day passed in a blur as I crossed Skyline Drive 11 times. Nearing the end of the day, I reached Possums Rest Overlook (2,300 ft.), which marks the northern boundary of SNP. After hiking nearly 20 miles, I arrived at the Tom Floyd Wayside Shelter (1,900 ft.) and set up my tent for the night.

Day 71—Tuesday, May 31, 2011—Week 11

I was in no hurry in the morning. I only needed to hike about three miles to reach VA 522, which led into Front Royal. When I reached the road, there was a fair amount of traffic. I began to hitch a ride. I was surprised that the man who picked me up was not at all familiar with the AT. He drove me about four miles and dropped me off at the Quality Inn about 10:00.

After I checked in, a friend, Bob Dowdy, arrived to spend the day with me. He had driven 180 miles from his home in Richmond to see me. Bob transported me first to the Post Office so that I could send home my stove and pan. I decided that I would no longer need to boil water for a hot meal at supper. I could get along fine with a main diet of cheese and peanut butter. Of course, I could purchase a hot meal whenever it was possible. As a result, my backpack would be lighter, and I would have more space. Making that decision gave me a feeling of confidence about being in control of my hike. During the day, Bob also drove me to a supermarket, laundromat, and to a restaurant for lunch and dinner. At a nearby hostel, I picked up the third care package sent from friends (Terea and Barry Kinney).

Day 72—Wednesday, June 1, 2011

Bob and I enjoyed a good breakfast at the motel, before he drove me back to the AT about 10:00. The day was warm, but the trail was pretty easy. At 5:00 I stopped to eat supper at the Manassas Gap Shelter (1,655 ft.), where I met two section hikers from Ohio. One man was the former Superintendent of Nordonia Hills City Schools in Northfield, and the other was a retired Judge from Bucyrus in Crawford County. Then I hiked another four miles before stopping about 8:00 to fill up my Camelbak with cold water from a spring. A few minutes later, I found a small campsite tucked in the woods just 15 yards off the trail and set up my tent for the night. I had hiked over 16 miles.

Day 73—Thursday, June 2, 2011

An absolutely beautiful day for hiking greeted me in the morning. It was breezy and in the seventies with low humidity. I stopped for lunch at the Rod

Hollow Shelter (840 ft.), which was .2 of a mile off the trail. I did not mind hiking that far off the trail to eat at a shelter. Shelters served as the most comfortable places to eat a meal because they usually had a picnic table. When it was raining, I was willing to hike farther than .2 of a mile to eat inside a dry shelter. Then I could still sit on the floor of a shelter and spread out the contents of my food bag.

There were spiders at the Rod Hollow Shelter, which were half the length of my index finger. I did not see spiders at any other shelter. As I left the shelter, I entered the 13.5-mile section of trail called the "roller coaster." That name was derived from a series of ten ascents and descents over viewless and rocky ridges. The difficulty was not in the length of each climb or descent, but in the ongoing change in direction. I was either climbing or descending.

When I saw a sign pointing 200 yards to the Bears Den Hostel in the early evening, I was pleased. It was a highly recommended hostel, and it lived up to its accolades. It was originally a stone mansion built in 1933 before it was recently restored. It is owned by the ATC but operated by the Potomac AT Club (PATC). I knew many of the 12 hikers staying. I was pleased to take advantage of the hiker special for $27.50, which included a bunk with linens, towel, and laundry facilities. The best part was that the price also included a large pizza, soda, and a pint of Ben and Jerry's ice cream.

Day 74—Friday, June 3, 2011

Pancakes were served for breakfast at the hostel. After I began hiking, I reached Snickers Gap (1,000 ft.) in about a half mile and said goodbye to the "roller coaster." A few minutes later, I saw a 1,000-mile marker nailed to a tree. I had planned to hike only eight miles to reach my destination for the day. About 1:00, I saw a sign pointing to the Blackburn Trail Center (1,400 ft.). A steep descent brought me to the property, which is owned and operated by the PATC. Hikers may stay at the hostel for free with donations accepted. It was once a privately-owned house with a great view of the country below. The caretaker told me that I could stay in the small bunkhouse or on the screened-in porch of the large house. I chose to sleep on the cooler porch to avoid snoring hikers. A free spaghetti dinner was provided, including a large brownie for dessert.

Day 75—Saturday, June 4, 2011

I left the Blackburn Trail Center early in the morning. It was located on the side of a mountain, just over a quarter mile below the AT. It took eight minutes and required climbing about 300 steps to get back to the trail. From there, I began a long descent toward Harpers Ferry, West Virginia.

As I was nearing West Virginia, I thought of the "24-Hour Challenge," which is attempted by a small number of hikers each year. The goal is to hike from the border of Virginia through West Virginia, Maryland, and into Pennsylvania in one calendar day. A hiker typically starts about midnight to have enough time to hike the nearly 50-mile distance within one day. A hike of that nature is quite a feat, but it risks injury. I knew of a strong hiker who tried the challenge in 2011, suffered a knee injury, and had to go home. The 24-hour challenge was not something that I even considered. The distance was daunting, and hiking all night in darkness was dangerous as well as mentally and physically draining.

WEST VIRGINIA

I was happy to enter West Virginia after having completed hiking the AT in four states (GA, NC, TN & VA). I had hiked 550 miles through Virginia in 39 days. However, I wouldn't be in my fifth state of West Virginia for very long. When I reached U.S. 340, I crossed the Shenandoah River Bridge. I saw a few kayakers in the water below. At 11:30 I reached the headquarters of the ATC in Harpers Ferry (population 286). The ATC is the primary organization responsible for the stewardship of the trail and 250,000 acres of public land surrounding it. Most hikers stop at the ATC headquarters to sign the register and proudly have their photo taken to be counted among the current class of thru-hikers. My photo was #296 in the 2011 thru-hikers' album. It was fun to look through the album and see photos of hikers I had met on the trail.

After checking in at the Town's Inn Hostel, I met Half Tongue, a hiker from Cleveland. He had seriously bitten his tongue while eating. Although it was bleeding extensively, he was so hungry that it didn't stop him from continuing his meal. While I was hiking, I met at least a dozen hikers from Ohio. I heard that Ohio had the unofficial claim of the most thru-hikers of any of the 36 states not on the AT.

Day 76—Sunday, June 5, 2011

Each morning hikers have the opportunity to make pancakes on a grill at the Town's Inn Hostel. The pancakes that we made were very doughy. They did not rise or brown up like normal pancakes. A female hiker said the pancakes tasted like flour. At that moment, we realized what we thought was pancake mix in an unlabeled container was just plain flour.

I took a zero day and was excited because my wife (Nancy), two daughters (Michelle & Cindi), along with three of my grandsons (Evan 10, Ryan 8, & Bradley 3), were due to visit me at the Comfort Inn in Harpers Ferry. I walked about a mile to the motel and checked in about 10:30. Soon my family arrived.

A family visit at Harpers Ferry, WV

Nancy said she would not have known me with my full and fuzzy beard if we had simply passed on the street. It had been nearly three months since I had shaved or had a haircut.

Cindi drove all of us to the ATC headquarters to view my photo on file. We returned to the Comfort Inn and had a picnic lunch at the gazebo. After lunch, we all hiked on the trail for a short distance. We stopped at Jefferson Rock, which overlooks where the Potomac and Shenandoah Rivers meet. The large rock was named to honor President Thomas Jefferson who was inspired by the beautiful view from there in 1783. In the afternoon, I was driven to a supermarket to resupply.

When we all returned to the motel, it was time for the highlight of the day for my grandsons. They took turns shaving my head and my beard with an electric clipper. The transformation was startling as I was left with a buzz cut and smooth face. When I looked in the mirror after the facial and head scalping, I saw a stranger. Afterwards, we all went out and enjoyed pizza for supper. At the end of the day, I reflected on what a fun day I had with my family and how it served to rejuvenate me.

Day 77—Monday, June 6, 2011

After breakfast at the motel, all of my family members took turns putting on my loaded backpack. It weighed nearly 40 pounds, as it had my recent food purchases as well as enough water to last the day. They all commented how heavy it felt. Then I was driven to the edge of town to resume the hike. Saying goodbye was a bittersweet moment. I knew that I would not see them for three or more months, but I was eager to resume my hike.

MARYLAND

Within a few minutes, I crossed the footbridge over the Potomac River and entered Maryland. I had completed hiking the AT in five states (GA, NC, TN, VA and WV) with nine states to go. For the first three miles into Maryland, the AT followed the C & O Canal Towpath, which is used also by those riding bicycles. Until 1924, this path was used by mules to tow barges in the canal. The trail was shaded, smooth, and flat. I thought how nice it would be if the trail were like that all the way to Maine. Dream on!

The trail eventually ascended about 800 feet. When I reached the Ed Garvey Shelter (1,100 ft.), I stopped for lunch. In the afternoon, the trail was often quite rocky, but thankfully the ascents and descents weren't steep for the most part. My feet were happy about that! After hiking about 18 miles, I arrived at the Dahlgren Backpacker Campground about 6:00. I set up my tent on a gravel tent pad. Most of the hikers camping there were section hikers. The state of Maryland operates this campground with no fees for hikers. There is a picnic table on each tent pad, and there is a bathroom with hot showers on the property. Luxury at its best!

To prevent a bear from stealing the food of a hiker, there was a sturdy 12-foot pole cemented into the ground with several hooks at the top to hang food bags. Getting a food bag onto a hook at the top of the stationary pole was difficult. A hiker needed to take his food bag and attach it to the end of a heavy 10-foot steel pole. The next step was to lift the 10-foot pole to reach a hook on the stationary pole. It took arm strength and dexterity to maneuver the food bag onto a hook. When I finally succeeded, I was both relieved and weary!

Day 78— Tuesday, June 7, 2011— Week 12

I began hiking at 7:00, and in a few miles I reached the Washington Monument State Park (1,550 ft.). On the grounds is the first monument that was built to honor President George Washington. The bottle-shaped stone tower is 34-feet tall and was dedicated by the citizens of Boonsboro, Maryland, on July 4, 1827. The monument was added to the National Register of Historic Places in 1972. Of course, when most people think of the Washington Monument, they think of the one in Washington, D.C. That 555-foot marble obelisk on the National Mall was completed in 1884, 57 years after the one in Maryland.

In the morning, I saw my fourth black snake and in the afternoon my fifth. The latter was thick and about four-feet long. Both of them slithered off the trail without me intervening. I ate lunch at the Pogo Memorial Campsite (1,500 ft.). Immediately after lunch, I found a shady spot to take a nap. I awoke after an hour, and the shade had dissipated as I was lying in the sun. However, the restful nap was exactly what I needed. After hiking about 19 miles, I reached the Raven Rock Shelter (1,480 ft.). I set up my tent about 6:30.

Day 79— Wednesday, June 8, 2011

I began hiking at 7:00. After hiking about an hour, I came to the PenMar County Park (1,330 ft.). I had the grounds completely to myself as no one was in sight. I bought a soda out of a vending machine and sat at a picnic table in the shade of trees for a short rest. After resuming my hike, I saw a sign marking the Mason-Dixon Line, the Maryland/Pennsylvania border.

PENNSYLVANIA

I was pleased to have completed hiking the AT in six states (GA, NC, TN, VA, WV and MD) with eight states to go. I had completed hiking 40 miles in Maryland in a little over two days. The ATC reports the two easiest states to hike in are West Virginia and Maryland, which were now both behind me. I did not look forward to hiking in my seventh state, Pennsylvania, where the trail covers about 230 miles. Most hikers do not like hiking there, because of the near constant rocky terrain. I heard Pennsylvania referred to as Rocksylvania. The trail was often simply a pile of rocks making it slow going, mentally tiring, and impossible to keep a consistent pace.

It was like walking on egg shells of all sizes. Watching where to place my foot on every step was absolutely necessary. At the end of nearly every day of hiking, the bottoms of my feet burned from the rough treatment they had withstood. A reasonable person would not have called the AT surfaces in Pennsylvania either a trail or footpath.

The typical rocky trail in PA

In late morning, I reached the Deer Lick Shelters, two nice shelters about 40 feet apart. One shelter's sign says "Snoring," while the other shelter's sign says "Non-Snoring." I did not see any other location where snorers were separated from non-snorers. I had lunch at the Antietam Shelter (890 ft.) in Old Forge Park. The day turned hot and humid with the temperature rising well above 90 degrees. It was largely uneventful, other than coping with the blistering heat and punishing rocks. In mid-afternoon, I stopped and changed my long pants to shorts and my long-sleeved shirt to a short-sleeved shirt.

At 7:00 I reached U.S. 30 and walked .3 of a mile to Taormina's Restaurant for dinner. I enjoyed a chocolate milk shake along with a calzone. I topped off my dinner with an ice cream cone for dessert. After walking back to the AT and crossing U.S. 30, I spotted a grassy area 25 feet off the AT and set up my tent just before dark. I was pleased to have hiked nearly 23 miles.

Day 80—Thursday, June 9, 2011

I started hiking bright and early about 5:45. To reach a highly recommended hostel for the night, I knew that I needed a full day of hiking. In a short time, I came to Caledonia State Park. I had trouble finding the white blazes in the area around the park and stopped twice to ask for directional help from local residents. I lost about a half hour getting myself back on the trail. I had lunch at the Birch Run Shelter (1,795 ft.), where I met a hiker from Mansfield, Ohio. I was elated when I got to the halfway point of the AT at 2:30. I was exactly 1,090.5 miles from both Springer Mountain in Georgia and Mt. Katahdin in Maine.

About 3:30, I reached PA 233, just south of the entrance to Pine Grove Furnace State Park. I had hiked over 19 miles. To celebrate having gone past the halfway point on the trail, some hikers take the "half-gallon challenge" at the Pine Grove General Store. The daunting task is to eat a half gallon of ice cream in one sitting! One hiker said he thought the challenge must have been a marketing ploy to sell a lot of ice cream. He may have been correct. I thought about giving it a try, but I wanted to be able to enjoy a pasta dinner at a hostel within the next two hours. I opted instead for an ice cream bar and soda.

The Ironmasters Mansion Hostel is right next to the general store. It is a recently renovated 1827 mansion that once served as a station on the Underground Railroad. After a very hot day of hiking, the air-conditioned hostel was a real treat and offered a good value for $27.50. I got to sleep in a bed, take a shower, and enjoy a pasta dinner, which was included in the cost of the stay.

Day 81—Friday, June 10, 2011

For breakfast, hikers enjoyed a plate of pancakes, which was also included in the cost of the stay. After breakfast, I visited the Appalachian Trail Museum. It was just a short distance down the road from the hostel. The museum is not large, but it contains some interesting memorabilia. I especially enjoyed seeing the Keds canvas tennis shoes and home-made rucksack carried by Emma (Grandma) Gatewood on her AT hikes. She thru-hiked the AT in 1955 at age 67. Then she did it again in 1960 at age 72. Finally, she completed a section hike of the AT in 1963 at age 75.

I thought of a few similarities I shared with Grandma Gatewood. We were both from Ohio, and we both attempted our first thru-hike of the AT at age 67. However, Grandma Gatewood slept on the ground on top of a shower curtain or perhaps under it, if it rained. I had a nice tent, air mattress, and sleeping bag. So much for the good old days!

During most of the day, the change in elevation was very moderate. However, the heat, humidity, and rocks made for a difficult hike! I felt tired after lunch, so I took a nap for an hour in the shade. In the late afternoon, I walked next to fields of corn and wheat before reaching Boiling Springs (population 2,982). After I ate dinner at a restaurant in town, I began to walk down PA 174 toward the Allenberry Resort Inn and Playhouse. Then I experienced trail magic once again. I was about half way to the inn when a hiker and his family saw me. The driver of the car made a U-turn, picked me up, and drove me to the inn. I

Grandma Gatewood's AT gear

did not know the hiker in the car, but he wanted to help me. He asked his father to turn around and drive out of his way to help me. It was an example of how supportive AT thru-hikers are to each other.

I was aware that the Allenberry Resort Inn was a good and inexpensive place for hikers to stay. The posted rate was nearly $160, but the hiker rate was only $40. As I registered, a middle-aged man who was standing near the front desk began to talk with me. He said the owners of the inn were friends of his family. To deal with the recession of the last few years, the owners decided to offer thru-hikers an inexpensive place to stay. Getting $40 for a room was better for the resort than the room remaining empty. Although it was not a big money maker for the owners, it allowed them to avoid having to lay off any long-term staff, so it was a win-win situation.

Day 82—Saturday, June 11, 2011

Included in the $40 price of the room was a delicious and extensive breakfast buffet. I left the inn with a full stomach, walked back ten minutes to the trail, and started hiking at 9:00. The hike had two distinct parts. The first dozen or so miles were mostly flat as the trail went through farmlands where corn, wheat, and soybeans were growing. Some fields were just uncut grass about chest high with the trail only the width of my body. It was warm, but I enjoyed the shade of nearby trees for part of the day.

As I was eating lunch at the Darlington Shelter (1,170 ft.), a hiker arrived. His trail name was Pilgrim, and he was from South Carolina. We talked just briefly before he resumed his hike. I went into the shelter for a nap. I slept for a little over an hour on a wooden bunk built into the shelter. Most shelters don't have bunks as hikers simply sleep on the floor of the shelter.

The second part of the day was over sharp and uneven rocks. In the early evening, I saw the Susquehanna River below the trail as it wound through Duncannon (population 1,508). After an extremely steep descent of about 30 minutes, I reached Market Street and entered the town about 7:30. I wanted to seek cover soon as the sky was blackening, and a severe thunderstorm appeared imminent.

After a quick stop to resupply at the convenience store of a service station, I resumed hiking and reached the Doyle Hotel about 8:00. I sat down on a stool in the bar and ordered what was called a "hearty haddock dinner" on the menu. It was delicious and filling. Sitting next to me was Delaware Dave, a gregarious, upbeat thru-hiker, whom I did not know previously.

I had already determined that I was not going to rent a room for the night. The hotel and town in general had seen better days. The Doyle was more than 100 years old, and most hikers did not have many good things to say about staying there. After eating a fine meal, I pushed on in the darkness, following the trail through town.

In about a mile, I reached the Riverfront Campground, but the office was closed for the night. I decided to set up my tent near the restrooms, which had an outside light. I was thrilled when I determined that I had hiked nearly 26 miles, a new personal record that I guessed would not be broken the rest of the hike. Train tracks were less than a hundred yards from my tent, and I heard a few trains during the night. One was so loud that it seemed like it was only feet away and headed in my direction. It gave me the eerie feeling that it would likely pass right through the middle of my tent.

Day 83—Sunday, June 12, 2011

I was awake by daybreak. Before leaving in the morning, I waited several minutes for the office to open, so that I could pay my bill for the campsite. After a short walk, I arrived about 8:00 at a Pilot Truck Stop and had breakfast. Then I began to hike across the Clarks Ferry Bridge, which spans the Susquehanna River. I kept an eye on a bird that took several passes close to my head. I imagine that it had a nest on the side of the bridge and mistook me for a possible predator. I was glad to have finally crossed the bridge with no injuries.

Leaving most trail towns is difficult as a hiker's pack is heavier after having resupplied with food. Furthermore, most trail towns are surrounded by mountains, and they require ascents upon leaving. In leaving Duncannon (385 ft.), there was a good deal of climbing, so up and up I went, sweating profusely.

In the early afternoon, I reached a parking lot at PA 225. I stopped to enjoy trail magic—a candy bar and cold soda. As I was finishing, Pilgrim arrived. I had met him briefly the day before. As he began to enjoy his soda and candy bar, I resumed hiking. The trail descended about a hundred yards before it leveled off.

Within a few minutes, a light rain began to fall. I stood under a tree, hoping that it was just a rain shower, which I had experienced several times on the trail. Suddenly, it began to rain harder, and I opened my backpack to find my pack cover. I took most of my gear out of my pack. No luck! It was the only time on the trail that I could not find my pack cover. Within a minute, the rain turned into a torrential downpour. Hail was pelting me, and rain was coming down in buckets.

Soon Pilgrim appeared wearing his rain jacket, and his backpack was covered. After a brief exchange, he kept hiking. I thought about hiking ahead three miles to a shelter. However, I decided that the wisest thing was to retreat to the parking lot at PA 225. As I walked back, going uphill, water was over the top of my boots. The trail had turned into a raging creek. Within a minute, I was cold and thoroughly soaked.

When I reached the parking lot, there were only four cars there. I walked by the first three cars and did not see anyone. In the last car were a man and woman I had seen a short time before on the trail. The man (Rick Steele) rolled down his window slightly as I said, "Do you know if there is a motel in this area?" He answered, "I don't know. I'm not from right around here, but I'll find one for you." Then he added, "Get in!" I threw my backpack on his back seat and jumped in. I said, "I'm sorry for getting your car so wet!" He immediately replied, "Don't worry. It's only water. It'll dry." As Rick began to drive, it was raining so hard that his windshield wipers were only marginally effective. He drove me several miles to a new Day's Inn in Harrisburg. We arrived at the motel about 2:15, and the rain continued to come down heavily. I felt as if I had been saved from drowning! I thanked Rick for his kind generosity in getting me to the motel.

What I thought was a dreadful day was about to turn into a blessing! I set up my tent in the room to dry out, showered, dried my boots, did my laundry, charged my phone, made calls to loved ones, used the free internet service, enjoyed an NBA playoff game on television, and ate dinner nearby at a fast-food restaurant.

In the evening, I called Mary Parry, aka Trail Angel Mary. Her name and phone number were shown in the *Appalachian Trail Thru-Hiker's Companion*. Mary lives in Duncannon and is willing to answer questions and provide help to thru-hikers. She agreed to pick me up at the motel the next morning and drive me back to the parking lot at PA 225. Before going to bed, I was amazed at the abrupt turn of events of the day. Although I had hiked only nine miles, I was delighted with the day's outcome. I was amazed at what seemed to me to be perhaps the worst day I experienced on the trail turned out to be among the most satisfying— thanks to Rick Steele and the trail magic he provided!

Day 84—Monday, June 13, 2011

I enjoyed a delicious complimentary breakfast at the motel. Trail Angel Mary arrived by 7:30 to drive me back to the trail on a cool but dry day. I was hiking by 8:00 and feeling completely refreshed. However, I noticed on several occasions that soon after a heavy rain there were cobwebs across the trail. Spiders were reestablishing their means to trap prey. When I could see the cobwebs ahead, I used my hiking sticks to clear the way. It was especially annoying when I couldn't see the cobwebs, and they hit me in the face.

It was a relatively easy day of hiking. The highest climb was 1,100 feet to the top of Stony Mountain (1,650 ft.). I napped for an hour in mid-afternoon along the trail. Then I hiked until 7:00 and camped just before Rausch Gap Shelter (970 ft.). I had covered 20 miles.

Day 85—Tuesday, June 14, 2011—Week 13

I began hiking on a cool day just before 8:00. The trail was relatively easy for the second day in a row. As I was crossing a small bridge in mid-morning, I noticed a lovely waterfall on the left. I thought how beautiful the whole area was with the trees, sunlight, and waterfall. As I got over the bridge, I was still appreciating the whole scene in my mind.

Unfortunately, I missed seeing the white blaze 30 feet off to the right, just after crossing the bridge. I continued walking on the crushed-stone road thinking how few scenes on the trail had affected me in such a positive way. As I continued hiking, I thought how nice it was to be on a flat surface, which I believed was the trail. About 15 minutes later, I realized that I had not seen a white blaze for quite a while. I thought that the road I was walking on had to be the trail. After hiking for a few more minutes, I decided to double back. Once again I realized how easy it was to have missed seeing where the trail turned. My frustration rose as I thought how I had hiked more than 30 minutes out of my way.

When I reached PA 72 about 11:30, I began to try to hitch a ride about three miles to Lickdale to resupply and have lunch. Traffic on the road was very light. After several minutes, a pickup truck driven by an older man went by me going in the opposite direction. Out of the blue, I yelled out, "I'll give you $10 to drive me to Lickdale." Suddenly the truck stopped and turned around. The driver was pleasant and found my hiking story interesting. He drove me a few miles to the convenience store of a service station. While I resupplied, he waited in his truck. When I got back to the trail in about 25 minutes, I gave the driver $10—money well spent. Then I sat under a shade tree and ate my lunch.

At 5:00 I stopped at the William Penn Shelter (1,300 ft.) to rest. I was surprised that no hikers were there. After I slept about an hour, I was back on the trail and reached the 501 Shelter (1,460 ft.) at 7:30. The shelter got its name because it is just a short distance from PA 501. It is one of only a few shelters on the trail that is enclosed. It has a long table, chairs, bunks, and a skylight. The structure once housed a potter who had her pottery wheel underneath the skylight. Potable water from a faucet and a solar shower are available at the adjacent caretaker's house.

When I arrived, seven hikers were sitting at the table eating dinner. I ordered a veggie stromboli and cheeseburger from an Italian restaurant that delivered to the nearby road. The only negative consequence of arriving last at the shelter was that the six lower bunks were taken, so I had to sleep on a top bunk. When I calculated my hiking distance for the day of over 17 miles, I realized that I had slightly less than 1,000 miles to go to reach Mt. Katahdin.

Day 86—Wednesday, June 15, 2011

In the morning, the temperature was in the low 50s. I was glad that I had been in the enclosed shelter overnight. My hands were cold as I began hiking. I wore two shirts and a jacket until I warmed up. In the morning, I stopped for a moment to observe a landscape in the distance when I heard someone behind me say hello. I turned and recognized Pilgrim. I had met him four days previously at the Darlington Shelter. Then I had seen him again briefly the following day when the severe thunderstorm knocked me off the trail. We talked for a few minutes about the storm and his decision to keep hiking. I explained how I was fortunate to have turned adversity into a great day.

Pilgrim had camped outside the 501 Shelter the night before while I stayed inside. When Pilgrim arrived at the shelter, there was only one hiker there. He did not know the hiker, but the man acted very strangely. Pilgrim decided to set up his tent to avoid the weird character. When I arrived, I also thought the hiker was peculiar. However, since there were six other hikers at the shelter, the man's behavior did not really concern me.

Pilgrim and I resumed hiking at the same time. I had hiked temporarily with numerous people for a period of time, ranging from a few minutes to several days. The only person I had previously committed to hiking with was Swamp Dawg. I liked the freedom and control of hiking by myself.

Elevation changes for the day were moderate. We experienced trail magic of a cold soda in the afternoon. Each time I discovered trail magic, my heartfelt thanks went out to whoever was responsible. Pilgrim and I were planning to stay at the Eagle's Nest Shelter, which was .3 of a mile off the AT. However, neither one of us saw any sign of it. When we reached Phillips Canyon Spring (1,500 ft.), we knew we were well past the shelter. After we got water from the spring down a steep ravine, we decided to camp just off the trail. We had hiked nearly 20 miles.

At dinner, I learned that Pilgrim's name was Lance Renault. He was from Greenville, South Carolina, and was nearly three years older than I. He was a long-distance section hiker and had completed half of the trail in 2010 with a hiking partner. Shortly before I met him, he had resumed hiking the trail at the halfway point in Pennsylvania. His goal was to reach Mt. Katahdin in 2011.

Day 87—Thursday, June 16, 2011

Pilgrim and I were on the trail by 6:30. We needed to hike just four miles to reach Port Clinton (population 279). Pilgrim had a reservation to stay at the Port Clinton Hotel. When we arrived at the old hotel about 8:00 in the morning, the doors were locked. It was to open later in the day. Even though the hotel was small, I wondered why it would not be open. Pilgrim was planning to resupply, do laundry, and use the computer at the local library. He asked me if I would consider spending the day in Port Clinton and sharing the cost of the hotel room, but I had no interest in doing that. After eating breakfast and resupplying, I was ready to get back on the trail.

We both were hungry, so we decided to walk about a half mile to the 3 C's Restaurant for a hearty breakfast. After we were done eating, I approached a man wearing a Phillies baseball cap sitting in a booth eating his breakfast. I told him I was an AT thru-hiker and wondered if he would be able to drive me to a supermarket when he was ready to leave. My boldness in approaching a total stranger and asking for a favor surprised me again. The man agreed to my request.

He drove me to a supermarket by mid-morning. While I resupplied, he had coffee and a donut. On the way back to the trail, the man said, "I gave a ride to two hikers, Dead Man and Padre, a few days ago." I did not know either hiker, but I hoped to meet them as I had seen their names in registers at shelters. Before I resumed hiking, I threw away the plastic wrap and cardboard on items I had just bought at the supermarket. Any excess or useless packaging takes up space and weight in a backpack. In the late afternoon, I took a break and had something to eat at the Windsor Furnace Shelter. As the threat of rain was looming, I set up my tent at a campsite along the trail at 6:45 after hiking 13 miles.

Day 88—Friday, June 17, 2011

The rain overnight delayed my start to 7:40. Early in the day, I reached The Pinnacle (1,615 ft.), which provides a beautiful panoramic view of Pennsylvania farmland. It was at moments like that when I fully appreciated the trail and wished everyone could see what I was seeing. After passing The Pinnacle, there were a descent and ascent of over 1,000-feet each. After lunch at the Allentown Hiking Club Shelter (1,350 ft.), I napped for an hour. When I awoke, I felt energized as usual!

In the afternoon, I listened to a cell phone message from a couple (Hardy and Elke Kaffenberger) who wanted to meet me on the trail the following afternoon. I called and told them I expected to be at PA 873/Lehigh Gap sometime in the late afternoon the next day. They would need to drive an hour and a half from their home in Kennett Square, Pennsylvania to get to Lehigh Gap. Then their plan was to hike south on the AT, until they met me heading north.

About 6:30, I reached PA 309. The Blue Mountain Restaurant was just a short walk down the road. As I entered the air-conditioned restaurant, I was sweaty, after having hiked nearly all day in very warm weather. While I was eating dinner, I tried unsuccessfully to charge my phone. I knew I needed to get to a Verizon store to fix my problem. It was absolutely essential to have a cell phone that worked. After dinner, I hiked another hour before setting up camp at 8:30 just off the AT. I had hiked about 19 miles.

Day 89—Saturday, June 18, 2011

I resumed hiking a little after 7:30. By mid-morning, I reached Bake Oven Knob (1,560 ft.), which is a big rock pile. Signage there leaves a lot to be desired. I spent about a half hour wandering around before I found a white blaze marking the trail. During the day, I spoke with two other hikers who also complained about the confusion caused where the trail was poorly marked.

I called Jerry Lehman, whom I had met on the trail in Virginia on May 5. Jerry had offered to visit me on the trail, if I made it to his area of Pennsylvania. I imagine he was surprised to hear from me. We arranged to meet two days later on Monday morning outside Wind Gap, Pennsylvania. During the afternoon, I fell on some rocks. I recalled what Swamp Dog had told me, "If you fall, try to fall on your backpack. It will absorb the shock." I did just that and was fine.

In the late afternoon, I saw a man approaching me on the trail. He was not carrying any type of backpack. After we exchanged glances, I said, "Hardy?" "Yes!" he answered. Then he immediately said, "I'm sorry that I didn't recognize you sooner!" I replied, "I fully understand. After all, I didn't exactly look like this when you last saw me." As we walked down the trail, Elke soon appeared. I was impressed that both of my friends had walked the trail to meet me. When we reached Lehigh Gap at PA 873, we got into their car. They drove me a few miles to an Italian restaurant and treated me to dinner. Then they drove me back to the trail, and we said our good byes.

I was back hiking about 5:30 in the evening. I crossed the bridge over Lehigh Gap (380 ft.) and tried to find my way up Blue Mountain (1,580 ft.). I suffered severe frustration again, as the blazes I followed disappeared before I could start up the mountain. I spent nearly 45 minutes in vain. Finally, I spotted a young man who had just descended the mountain and was getting into his car to leave. He told me where to find the trailhead, which had been relocated.

I began the steep, rugged and dangerous 1,200-foot climb up Blue Mountain. Since there were no trees, the blazes were painted on rocks. Some blazes were easy to spot, and some weren't. When I was almost to the top, I lost sight of any blazes. I walked around in the very treacherous area to no avail. I decided my best option was to descend the mountain.

Blue Mountain in the Lehigh Valley of PA

After I had hiked down the mountain for several minutes, I noticed a blaze well off to my right. I decided to attempt to get over the mountain one more time. Thank goodness, I succeeded that time. As I looked back at Lehigh Gap before beginning my descent on the other side of the mountain, I admired the panoramic view. I saw vegetation that had been destroyed as a result of nearly a century of zinc smelting in Palmerton, Pennsylvania (population 5,414). The Environmental Protection Agency shut down the smelting furnaces in 1980. The affected area was put on the Superfund clean-up list in 1982. The mountain is slowly coming back to life and efforts to bring back vegetation are ongoing.

I hiked until 8:30. As I was setting up my tent, I could see homes and buildings that were a long distance below in Palmerton. Before I went to sleep, I read in the *Appalachian Trail Thru-Hiker's Companion* that the rock scramble up Blue Mountain was among the most challenging on the AT, south of New Hampshire. I would fully agree, as it was not for the faint of heart! Although I had been severely confused twice about the location of the trail, I still managed to hike 15 miles during the difficult 13-hour day.

Day 90—Sunday, June 19, 2011

I awoke very early on Father's Day. I thought of my own father, Charles. He died suddenly in 1960 at age 54 of an aortic aneurysm. I was a sophomore in high school and just short of my 16th birthday. He was well liked and loved by family and friends alike. I wish that I would have had the opportunity to spend time with him as an adult.

In the morning, a giant cloud completely obscured the town below. I began hiking at 7:00, and by mid-morning I was out of water. As I approached Little Gap (1,100 ft.) at Blue Mountain Road, I planned to try to hitch a ride into town, where I could get water. A few hundred yards before reaching the road, I saw two hikers who were sitting next to their tent about 50 feet off the trail. I said, "Hello, do you have any water?" One camper replied, "Yes, we do. We're fine. We have water." He failed to understand that I was hoping he would offer me some. I said, "O.K." and moved on. I hiked about 30 yards when I heard one of the men I had passed yell out, "Would you like some water?" I turned and said, "Sure, if you can spare some!"

I walked back to near the campsite, and one of the men brought a large jug of water to me. He said, "My cousin and I are leaving in a few hours to go home, and we won't need this water. We're drinking beer!" He proceeded to fill my Camelbak with about two liters of water. His generosity meant that I did not have to leave the trail at Little Gap. After we spoke for a few minutes, I could tell that he was feeling no pain. Then I understood how the beer had resulted in his misunderstanding of my initial inquiry!

After I had lunch sitting on a large flat rock just off the trail, I needed a nap. I spread my Tyvek ground cover on the rock, used my clothes bag for a pillow, and slept for one hour and twenty minutes. I heard a few hikers passing by, but moments later I was back asleep. I was amazed that one of my longest naps on the trail happened on a large flat boulder! I remembered that my wife had said more than once, "You could sleep on a bed of nails!" Maybe she was right!

I stopped for dinner at Leroy Smith Shelter (1,410 ft.). As I was eating supper, Pilgrim arrived. I had last seen him in Port Clinton three days before. After dinner, he stayed in the shelter, but I continued hiking three miles farther. I

Flat rock in PA where I ate lunch and napped

camped 20 yards off the trail. I was less than two miles from the road outside Wind Gap, where I was to meet Jerry Lehman the next morning between 7:00 and 7:30.

Day 91, Monday, June 20, 2011

I was up before 5:00 a.m. and began hiking by 6:00. I didn't eat anything because I knew I would have breakfast with Jerry. It had been six weeks since I had first met him while he was section hiking in Virginia. About 6:30, I got to PA 33 where we planned to meet. I was pleased because I did not want Jerry to arrive first and not find me. I truly appreciated Jerry's kind offer to drive an hour from his home to meet me and help me out. While I waited, I reviewed my upcoming itinerary.

Jerry arrived about 7:00. It was only a mile into Wind Gap (population 2,720), where we ate breakfast at the Gap Diner. Then I was able to do my laundry, resupply at a supermarket, and buy a new charger for my cell phone. It was quite a productive morning, and Jerry was fantastic in shuttling me around to complete all my chores. Finally, he drove me back to the trail, and I resumed hiking at 11:00 feeling contented. My hiking goal for the rest of the day was to complete 16 miles. The changes in elevation were moderate, except for the 1,100-foot descent into Delaware Water Gap (population 746). At 7:45 I arrived at my destination, The Presbyterian Church of the Mountain Hostel.

I immediately met two hikers I knew, sitting outside the entrance of the hostel. They raved about the chicken pot pie and small fruit pie they had eaten at a local business, which was about ten minutes away. They advised me to go immediately to the Bakery & Farmers Market, because it was closing at 8:00. I took their advice, and got there just before it closed. I bought a chicken pot pie, a small peach pie, and a drink. As I sat at a picnic table outside the store and enjoyed my dinner, I was grateful for the hikers' suggestion.

Then I walked back to the hostel and went inside. It was packed, so I set up my tent in the backyard. Pilgrim arrived and set up his tent about 30 feet away from me. He told me he had fallen on the trail, cut his head, and injured his ribs.

Day 92—Tuesday, June 21, 2011—Week 14

There was a light rain overnight, but it had stopped by morning. I strolled to the DWG Diner about a half mile away and enjoyed a leisurely breakfast. Then I walked down the street to an outfitter, The Pack Shop. Due to rough treatment from the sharp and cutting rocks in Pennsylvania, the titanium tips on my hiking sticks had broken off. I bought new ones, which were installed by the shop owner. I felt confident that once more I had hiking sticks which would keep me upright.

When I returned, Pilgrim was still at the hostel. He was taking a zero day to rest from the injuries which he had suffered. Since I had gone to breakfast and to the outfitter, I didn't begin hiking until about 10:45. It was a very short walk to the Delaware River Bridge, which marks the border between Pennsylvania and New Jersey.

NEW JERSEY

After crossing the bridge, I had completed my AT hike in seven states (GA, NC, TN, VA, WV, MD and PA) with seven states to go. I would need to hike about 72 miles to get through New Jersey, where the rocks were only slightly less numerous than in Pennsylvania.

In the afternoon, I saw a small snake, which was starting to cross the trail. It turned and within just a few seconds completely vanished into the underbrush. Several times later on the trail, I saw these small but very quick-moving racer snakes. During the day there were two young section hikers, who were either slightly ahead or behind me, depending on when we took breaks. They saw a black bear with two cubs as well as a rattlesnake. None of the animals caused any problem for the hikers. From my own experience, I realized how an animal can appear on the trail and then quickly disappear. After I hiked nearly 14 miles, I set up camp about 6:15 near Rattlesnake Spring (1,260 ft.).

Day 93 — Wednesday, June 22, 2011

It rained heavily overnight, resulting in a soggy campsite in the morning. The bottom of my tent was damp on the inside from sitting on the wet ground. Although I didn't like the dampness, I was used to dealing with it. The hardest thing was packing my tent when it was both wet and muddy. I dealt with that by putting it into a plastic grocery bag, so that my gear would remain reasonably dry and clean.

I was hiking by 8:00, and I stopped a few times to munch on small but sweet wild blueberries. It took about 20 berries to make a small handful. The rain returned several times, making the trail slick. I fell a few times on the wet rocks and roots. Thankfully, my most severe injury was a small abrasion below my thumb.

I stopped for water at the Brick Road Shelter. I had been warned by another hiker of a huge problem with mosquitoes there. The warning was accurate. The good news was that the water was from a spring and didn't need treatment. The bad news was that I had never seen mosquitoes as thick any other time on the trail. There were so many swarming mosquitoes I feared that my blood could be sucked dry before I finished getting a couple of liters of water from the spring. I kept moving my body and flailing my arms to ward off the critters. After I got away from the mosquitoes, I was surprised to have suffered only a few bites. It was the only time on the trail when any flying insects were a major problem. I carried a small spray bottle of 100% deet to use when needed to protect against mosquitoes.

After hiking about 15 miles, I arrived in the late afternoon at U.S. 206/Culvers Gap. Just a short distance down the road was Kevin's Steakhouse, where I ate an early dinner about 4:30. There were only a few other people in the restaurant. The television was on, and a weather forecast predicted severe thunderstorms and a possible tornado overnight. Hearing that, I decided that staying indoors was the best alternative.

After dinner, the restaurant owner's wife kindly drove me and another hiker to the Forest Motel. It was about four miles down the road in Branchville. It was an older structure, and not one that I would recommend. My room was small and dingy, and the motel did not even have an ice machine. The lack of ice at a motel may not be a crime, but certainly it should be enough reason to file a civil suit against the owner!

Day 94, Thursday, June 23, 2011

It appeared the nasty weather was over in the morning. The manager of the motel drove another hiker and me back to the trail. The cost for the short ride was

$10, which we split. We stopped and had breakfast at a small deli—Joes to Go. It was just a hop, skip and jump from the AT.

After I began hiking, a light rain fell. I was hoping to get to the Gren Anderson Shelter (1,320 ft.) about two miles ahead to escape the rain. Within a few minutes, a downpour ensued. This time I was able to find and put on the cover over my backpack. I had my doubts that my gear would remain dry with such a heavy rain. I was soaked, and my feet sloshed inside my boots. When I reached the shelter, I opened my backpack and checked my gear. I was pleasantly surprised that nearly everything inside the pack had remained totally dry. Besides the pack cover, I had an industrial-strength garbage bag lining the inside.

I put on some dry clothes, talked to a few hikers at the shelter, and watched the constant rain for a while. Then I blew up my air mattress and climbed into my sleeping bag. I slept for well over an hour. When I awoke, the rain had stopped. One of the hikers who had been at the shelter when my nap started had moved on.

I pondered whether I should resume my hike. Since it was only mid-afternoon, I put on my wet clothes and resumed hiking about 3:00. A few times I spotted small yellow salamanders on the trail. At 7:00 I found a nice campsite on a ridge just past the Rutherford Shelter (1,345 ft.). I set up my tent with the threat of rain once again in the air. Considering the long delay and stormy weather, I was satisfied with having hiked about 12 miles. I wasn't in my tent long when the rain began to fall again.

Day 95—Friday, June 24, 2011

In the morning, I was greeted by a mist and a heavy fog that blanketed the trail. After I started to hike, I experienced a series of moderate ascents and descents. In mid-morning I reached the High Point State Park (1,803 ft.) and saw its 220-foot monument. It marks the highest point in the state of New Jersey. I entered the monument and spoke with a young woman, who was sitting at a desk reading a book. She said that I was the first visitor of the day. I could certainly see why as visibility was extremely limited. It was impossible even to see the top of the monument. On a clear day, a visitor can see a spectacular panorama of farmland and forest in three states. I could only imagine seeing breathtaking views of the Pocono Mountains to the west and Catskill Mountains to the north.

After taking a short break, I resumed hiking. Within five minutes, confusion reigned yet again, as the white blazes disappeared. After I eventually found my way, I pondered if I was directionally challenged or was the trail lacking proper signage. Although I was certainly willing to take the blame on some occasions, this time the trail was the primary culprit.

The trail skirted the NJ/NY line. In the afternoon, I hiked nearly a half mile into in Unionville, New York (population 561). I had a calzone for lunch at

Annabel's Pizza and resupplied at Horler's Store. As I was putting my groceries into my backpack, a man stopped to talk. For many years, he had worked at a well-known hostel called the Mayor's House in Uniontown. The hostel got its name because the mayor offered thru-hikers the opportunity to sleep in his basement. I asked why the Mayor's House was no longer a hostel. He said it was because the mayor, who had retired, was a widower and was getting remarried. He determined that his new bride would not want to house smelly and dirty hikers every night for many months each year. It wasn't hard for me to understand that reasoning!

The rest of the day was uneventful, and the weather improved. However, I felt a burning sensation on the bottoms of my feet from hiking on the rocky trail. After hiking about 17 miles, I reached the Pochuck Mountain Shelter (840 ft.) at 6:30. There were six section hikers there, and all of them were camped in tents. When it was close to dark, there were still no hikers in the shelter, which slept six. I decided to set up my tent inside the shelter to be sure to remain dry and ward off mosquitoes. There was plenty of room for any late hiker arrivals, but none arrived!

Day 96—Saturday, June 25, 2011

I was pleased in the morning because the recent weather had changed dramatically for the better. The sun was shining, and I got a late start about 9:00. The trail went through a lengthy stretch of wetlands. I walked for more than a mile on boardwalks and then on wooden planks for at least another mile.

After hiking about seven miles, I reached NJ 94. Crossing the road and walking about 100 yards on the trail, I met a southbound section hiker. He was on his way to the St. Thomas Episcopal Church Hostel in Vernon, New Jersey. He had heard it was a very nice place that offered a lot of amenities. I also had heard good things about the hostel. We parted company, and I continued hiking north. Within a few minutes, I rethought my decision. I really liked the benefits of what the hostel could offer, as well as giving my feet time to rest.

I turned around and headed back to NJ 94. Vernon was less than three miles down the road. A local man picked me up and drove me into Vernon. I asked him to drop me off at the Dairy Queen for lunch. I was soon slurping a large chocolate milk shake and eating a chicken sandwich. Then I walked ten minutes to the hostel. It was early afternoon, and the few hikers still there were taking a zero day. I showered, did laundry, used the computer, charged my phone and camera, and dried my boots and tent in the sun.

In the late afternoon, Pilgrim arrived. He and I decided to go to an Italian restaurant for dinner and then resupply at a supermarket. We had just placed our pizza order when Portrait walked in. He accepted our offer to join us at our table. I hadn't seen him for a while, and it was good to renew an old acquaintance. He was staying at the hostel as well.

Pilgrim and I agreed to hike together for the following day. I was not yet ready to commit to anything longer. As I settled down on my air mattress in my sleeping bag for the night, I was happy that I had decided to go to the hostel. Even though I had only hiked about seven miles, I had accomplished a lot and felt rested.

Day 97, Sunday, June 26, 2011

Pilgrim and I and a few other hikers attended the 8:00 Holy Eucharist Service at St. Thomas Episcopal Church. Immediately after church, a member of the congregation drove us back to the trail. The driver told us about the Bellvale Creamery, which had delicious ice cream. He said that we would be near the business later in the day after entering New York. We began hiking at 9:30 and ate lunch at the Wawayanda Mountain Shelter (1,200 ft.). There were many difficult climbs and rock scrambles during the day. In mid-afternoon, we reached a large flat rock which marked the NJ/NY State Line. The 72 miles through New Jersey had taken five-and-a-half days.

NEW YORK

I had completed hiking in eight states on the trail (GA, NC, TN, VA, WV, MD, PA and NJ) with only six states to go. In a half-mile, we reached Prospect Rock (1,433 ft.), the highest point on the AT in New York. Later In the afternoon, we reached NY 17A. We walked a quarter mile down the road to the Bellvale Creamery, which was packed. After I began eating my double-scooped cone, I could understand why the parking lot was full. The ice cream was absolutely fabulous, the best I had on the whole hike. Several days later, we were still joking about walking back to enjoy some ice cream at the Bellvale Creamery again. After eating, we walked a few more miles to the Wildcat Shelter (1,180 ft.) and set up camp after hiking over 17 miles.

Day 98—Monday, June 27, 2011

Pilgrim and I started hiking about 8:30. We faced many rock scrambles, and there were very few level areas on the trail. We were repeatedly climbing and then descending over and over again. It was very challenging physically and mentally. One place we climbed was appropriately called Agony Grind located on Arden Mountain. We took several breaks during the day, which were absolutely necessary.

In the late afternoon, we reached an interesting place called the Lemon Squeezer (1,150 ft.) in Harriman State Park. A hiker must squeeze through a very narrow section of rock, which is about two feet wide, twenty feet long, and angled. It's tricky to get through. Immediately after that, there is a scramble up a rock face. Pilgrim especially disliked that area and complained bitterly about it. On the other hand, I actually enjoyed the challenge that section offered.

The very narrow "Lemon Squeezer" in NY

After we reached the Fingerboard Shelter (1,300 ft.) at 5:45, we set up camp for the night. We were tired after hiking just over 14 miles.

Day 99—Tuesday, June 28, 2011—Week 15

We began hiking about 7:30. I decided to continue hiking with Pilgrim for the foreseeable future. Pilgrim and I got along fairly well, and our pace was similar. He was someone to talk with, and he could take a photo of me at times. In case of an emergency, either of us would be there to help the other. In the evening, we would collectively determine how far we hoped to hike the next day. We agreed that either of us could call for a break during the day. I especially enjoyed the fact that he would take the lead on the trail and be the primary person to look for white blazes. He was quite good at spotting the blazes, especially where the trail was not well marked. I was fed up with the confusion caused at times by the apparent absence of good signage necessary to keep me on the trail.

During the day, we experienced trail magic twice. After crossing two roads many miles apart, there were gallon bottles of spring water available for thru-hikers. Since there were no water sources on the trail for 12 miles, it was a perfect gift. I was delighted to fill my Camelbak with water that I did not need to treat.

We had lunch at the information center/bookstore of the Palisades International Parkway, which was nearly a half mile off the AT. As we sat eating lunch, a young man with the trail name of Arthur Dent arrived and sat down to join us. He was Jason Jones from Dover, Ohio. I did not know why he had chosen his trail name. I learned later that Arthur Dent was a fictional character in *The Hitchhiker's Guide to the Galaxy*, a comic science-fiction series. As we were finishing lunch, a man in a car stopped and talked to us briefly. He offered each of us a banana. It was an unusual gift of trail magic, but I enjoyed it.

Pilgrim and I arrived at the Bear Mountain Zoo just before 5:00. Thru-hikers are admitted free as the trail goes right through the zoo. The AT descends to 124 feet above sea level there, the lowest elevation on the trail. At the exit of the zoo is the Bear Mountain Bridge, a toll bridge for vehicles. When the first thru-hiker (Earl Shaffer) crossed the bridge in 1948, it cost him a nickel. However, it is now free for hikers.

Pilgrim and I temporarily parted company at the bridge. He continued hiking toward the Graymoor Spiritual Life Center, which was about seven miles ahead. He planned to stay at the Life Center, which is operated by the Franciscan Friars of the Atonement. It offers people of different religious traditions an opportunity to slow down and encounter the Spirit in their lives as well as retreats and programs designed for individuals and groups.

I had arranged with friends to meet me at the parking lot next to the bridge. Rosemary Burns arrived at 5:15 and drove me to her home in Cortlandt Manor, NY, where she lives with her husband, Artie. After a shower and wonderful dinner, Artie took me to a supermarket to resupply. Then I had the pleasure of enjoying a good night's rest in a comfortable bed.

Day 100—Wednesday June 29, 2011

In the morning, Artie drove me to where the AT meets the Graymoor Spiritual Life Center. Pilgrim was taking a zero day at the Life Center. I hiked back from there to the Bear Mountain Bridge, where Artie picked me up. This type of hike is called a flip-flop, since I was a northbound thru-hiker heading south on the trail. The plan was for both of us to resume hiking the next day from the Graymoor Spiritual Life Center.

After lunch, Artie drove me to West Point to tour the U.S. Military Academy. It is on the west bank of the Hudson River about 40 miles north of New

York City. I had always wanted to visit the Academy, and it was a real treat to see its most impressive grounds. Artie was a great tour guide. We walked on the football field, went inside the beautiful chapel and Eisenhower Hall Theater, saw the parade grounds, talked briefly with a few cadets, and toured the entire campus. In the evening, I visited with several of Artie and Rosemary's neighbors. It was a fun night as I spoke about my AT adventure and showed my photos from the trail on a large television screen.

Day 101—Thursday, June 30, 2011

In the morning, the Burnses drove me to Graymoor Spiritual Life Center (550 ft.), so I could meet Pilgrim. I really appreciated the Burns' hospitality and all they did for me during my visit. We began hiking at 8:30, and an hour later we found trail magic of cold sodas. It was a pretty easy day of hiking, as the highest elevation of the day was at Shenandoah Mountain (1,282 ft.). However, I faced a new problem on the hike; a toe on my left foot began to throb. After hiking about 19 miles, I was relieved when we reached the RPH Shelter (360 ft.) at 5:45. The shelter was the size of a one-car garage. The door was near the trail, but the rear of the building was open sided. There was a concrete patio with a picnic table behind the shelter. The water source was an old hand pump. It looked antiquated, but after several hard pumps, the water flowed rapidly. As I started to set up my tent on the grass, a hiker advised me that I should avoid camping on grass whenever possible, due to the possibility of ticks. I took his advice seriously, so I moved to an area of sandy soil and set up my tent. From that point on, I tried to avoid setting up my tent on grass.

At the shelter, I met a friendly and likeable hiker named Old Granddad, whose real name is Dave Howell. He had attempted to thru-hike the trail in 2010, but he suffered from plantar fasciitis and could not complete his trek. He had recently returned to continue his hike.

Dave told me how he had chosen his trail name. When Dave's wife, Kitty, became pregnant, his father, Doyle, received a bottle of Old Grand-Dad Bourbon Whiskey to remind him of his advanced stage in life. When Doyle's grandson, Dale, was born in 1969, Doyle and Dave shared a shot of the bourbon. On Dale's 21st birthday, all three men had a shot of the whiskey. When Doyle died in 1999, Dave, Dale, and other relatives finished off the original bottle of Old Grand-Dad in honor of Doyle's life. It took 30 years of significant events in Doyle's life for the original bottle to be consumed.

A year later, Dale surprised Dave with the original bottle of Old Grand-Dad, but it was filled with Scotch, Dave's alcohol of choice. A new round of celebration began when Dale's daughter, Delena, was born in 2001. That meant that Dave was then the new "Old Granddad." Although Dave favors Scotch, he decided to carry a very small bottle of Old Grand-Dad on the AT to drink in celebration upon summiting Mt. Katahdin.

100

Day 102—Friday, July 1, 2011

It was cool and dry as we began hiking at 7:00. As we ate lunch at the Morgan Stewart Shelter (1,285 ft.), we determined that we would camp at the Telephone Pioneer Shelter (910 ft.) about eight miles ahead. Since I felt very tired, I decided to nap after lunch. Pilgrim continued hiking, and I slept for about 45 minutes. When I resumed hiking, I went at a slower pace, and my sore toe felt much better. I hiked along the shore of Nuclear Lake, which was the site of a facility to process nuclear fuels until 1972. About 4:30, I arrived at the shelter. Pilgrim had set up his tent and was resting, and I set up camp near him. I was pleased to have hiked about 17 miles.

Day 103—Saturday, July 2, 2011

My toe felt better in the morning. We began hiking by 7:30 and soon passed the Dover Oak. It is reportedly the largest oak tree on the AT and is estimated to be over 300 years old. Next we reached the AT railroad station at NY 22. A commuter train provides service from there to the Grand Central Station in New York City.

We crossed the railroad tracks and walked about a half mile down the road to Tony's Deli. A large cinnamon sweet roll and bottle of orange juice hit the spot. It was also a good time to resupply on a limited basis, as the store carried a fair variety of food. Pilgrim bought a pastrami sandwich on rye to go. Although he claimed to be a vegetarian while he was at home, he certainly liked pastrami on the trail.

After hiking for another seven miles, we stopped for lunch at the Wiley Shelter (740 ft.). Pilgrim gobbled down his pastrami sandwich, while I ate my typical lunch of peanut butter and Nutella on a bagel and cheese on a bagel. I began to think that perhaps I was more a vegetarian than Pilgrim! Since I no longer cooked on the trail, my typical breakfast and dinner did not vary much from my typical lunch. Surprisingly, I didn't tire of eating the same thing at nearly every meal. I tried many different varieties of cheese, and I liked all of them. The unrefrigerated cheese kept fairly well for up to four days even in the heat of summer.

CONNECTICUT

After lunch, we hiked a little more than a mile and saw a sign welcoming us to Connecticut. I had completed my AT hike through nine states (GA, NC, TN, VA, WV, MD, PA, NJ and NY) with five states to go. The AT only covers about 52 miles in Connecticut. A noticeable difference of early hiking in Connecticut versus New York was that the trail was less rocky. That was a welcome development for my feet. There were climbs of 600 feet and 1,050 feet. The highest elevation of the day was at the summit of Schaghticoke Mountain (1,331 ft.). From there we descended over two miles to the Schaghticoke Mountain Campsite (950 ft.). Since Connecticut restricts camping to designated sites, we set up our tents there. We had hiked 18 miles.

Day 104—Sunday, July 3, 2011

In the morning, we got an early start at 6:30 as we skipped breakfast. Unfortunately, the rocky terrain reappeared. We hiked a little over three miles to reach CT 341. We began to hitch a ride into Kent (population 2,979), which is in the northwest corner of the state. Its appeal is based on its charming and well-kept appearance. The downtown is a mix of residential homes, unique shops, art galleries, restaurants, and other businesses. As we began to hitch a ride, the first car stopped to pick us up. The driver was a woman about our age. She drove us a few miles into town and dropped us off at a restaurant along the main street. We ate a great breakfast sitting outside at a table along the sidewalk. I only went inside the restaurant to plug in the charger for my cell phone.

After breakfast, we walked down the street to the Davis IGA to resupply. Then we went to the Backcountry Outfitters. While we were there, Pilgrim signed us up to get a shuttle back to the trail for $10. I was surprised that we did not hitch a ride, but I was OK with his decision. About 11:00 we were back on the trail. Soon a light rain began to fall.

We stopped for lunch at the Stewart Hollow Brook Lean-to (425 ft.). What most other states call a shelter is called a "lean-to" in Connecticut. The rain increased in intensity and continued steadily all afternoon. We debated whether to stay at the lean-to or resume hiking. We decided to simply spend the rest of the day out of the rain in the lean-to. It made for a short hike of only 10 miles.

Day 105—Monday, July 4, 2011

Independence Day was dry and humid. I knew several hikers who were planning to be in NYC for the fireworks celebration. During the day, there were numerous climbs totaling over 2,000 feet, mostly on rocky terrain. Early in the day, Pilgrim fell on a wet tree root, and later I slipped on a muddy embankment. Thankfully, no one was injured. After hiking five hours and covering over 10 miles, we stopped for lunch at the Pine Swamp Brook Lean-to (1,075 ft.). In mid-afternoon, we climbed Mt. Easter (1,350 ft.), which was the highest elevation of the day. About 4:30, after hiking over 15 miles, we reached the Belter's Campsite (770 ft.), our home for the night.

While I was asleep in my tent, I heard the sound of an explosion and what sounded like discharges from a small firearm. It concerned me for several seconds. Then I thought of the logical reason for the loud and disturbing noises. Duh! It was the Fourth of July. I got out of my tent and rubbed my eyes. I could see remnants of exploding fireworks at a distance in the sky. Hail to the "land of the free and home of the brave."

Day 106—Tuesday, July 5, 2011—Week 16

We got an early start on a warm day. Our destination was Salisbury (population 1,363). We became puzzled as to the location of the trail after we reached U.S. 7/CT 112. As usual, we eventually got straightened around and made our way through Falls Village (population 538). By mid-morning, we climbed Prospect Mountain (1,475 ft.), the highest elevation of the day. After hiking over 10 miles, we reached Salisbury about 11:30.

We rented a double room for $35/person at the home of Vanessa Breton. We showered, ate lunch in the village courtyard, did our laundry, resupplied at LaBonne's Epicure Market, and used the internet at the library. Arthur Dent and GipCgirl, an older woman from Australia, were also staying at the Breton home. GipCgirl began thru-hiking the AT in 2010, before breaking her ankle in Georgia. After taking time to recover, she only made it to New England, as her visa expired. She could not get an extension to finish the hike. She returned in 2011 to hike the AT once again. Instead of starting in New England, where she had stopped in 2010, she began once again in Georgia. It was important for her to thru-hike the entire AT.

Day 107—Wednesday, July 6, 2011

We got a ride to the trail in the morning from Vanessa Breton's son, who was on his way to work. Since we had resupplied, our backpacks weighed about seven pounds more than when we entered Salisbury. The weather forecast was calling for a 90-degree day with possible thunderstorms. It didn't seem quite that hot, and we didn't experience any rain. We had two ascents of 1,000 feet and one of nearly 700 feet. In the late morning, we climbed Bear Mountain (2,316 ft.), the highest peak in Connecticut. Then we descended into Sages Ravine (856 ft.), a beautiful section of dark forest, steep hills, and rock.

MASSACHUSETTS

In the early afternoon, we saw a sign welcoming us to Massachusetts. It had taken about four-and-a- half days to hike 52 miles through Connecticut. I had completed my AT hike in ten states (GA, NC, TN, VA, WV, MD, PA, NJ, NY and CT) with four states to go. The AT covers about 90 miles in Massachusetts.

When it was time for lunch, we weren't near a shelter. We simply stepped off the narrow trail and sat under a small pine tree, which offered some shade. In the mid-afternoon, we climbed Mt. Everett (2,624 ft.), the second highest point in the Taconic Mountain range in Massachusetts. When we reached Glen Brook Lean-to (1,885 ft.) at 3:45, we set up our tents for the night. A benefit of stopping early to set up camp was that we could put wet items in the sun to dry. We often arrived at camp in the evening, when it was not as conducive to drying out wet things.

We had hiked only 14 miles. The main reason that we did not hike longer was that the next lean-to was over 14 miles ahead. There were no designated campsites within that area either. Terrain in the northern states is much more uneven and rocky than in the southern states. Especially in New England, there aren't many level spots, where a hiker can simply walk off the trail and find a good campsite. Since my AT journey began, I was pleased to have hiked over 1,500 miles.

Day 108—Thursday, July 7, 2011

We started hiking about 6:45 in order to get to MA 41, where Pilgrim had arranged for us to meet a couple about 8:00. Steve and Carol Ide picked us up there and took us to breakfast at Mom's Country Café in South Egremont. Steve and Carol had performed professionally with Arlo Guthrie for seven years. Steve played the guitar, and Carol sang. It was fun to talk with them and hear about their professional life. After we ate breakfast, we went to their home for a short visit. Before he drove us back to the trail, Steve was able to tighten the tips on my hiking sticks. Pilgrim and I enjoyed being with Steve and Carol and appreciated their hospitality.

After we resumed hiking, we soon reached Shays' Rebellion Monument (700 ft.). The stone marker commemorates the last bloody battle by farmers against government taxes and debt collection in 1787. Daniel Shays was an American Revolutionary War veteran who led the armed uprising and unsuccessful revolt. While we were walking by that area, we saw what looked like a farmer wearing a wide-brimmed hat, closely examining the plowed farm land. We thought that he was simply checking out the dry soil. We spoke briefly with him. The man was not a farmer, but merely a collector of artifacts. He was hoping to find a remnant of the last battle of the rebellion, which had occurred nearly 125 years before.

A little while later, we were delighted to find Gatorade in a cooler near a road. Once again, it was most appreciated, especially with the warm weather. During the day, the trail had many miles of boardwalks over wetlands. The highest elevation of the day was at the summit of East Mountain (1,800 ft.). After hiking over 14 miles, we reached the Tom Leonard Lean-to (1,540 ft.) and set up our tents about 5:45.

Day 109—Friday, July 8, 2011

The day began with a very overcast sky. Once again, we walked through several miles of wetlands. Pilgrim slipped on the boardwalk and stepped off, resulting in a soaker. After he uttered a few choice words, he was OK and resumed hiking. Sometimes the boardwalk over wetlands was wide, dry and easy to walk on. At other times it was narrow, wet, and slippery. When I stepped onto a boardwalk, it occasionally moved or even sunk inches under water. When walking on a boardwalk, a good rule was to expect the worst, but hope for the best.

There were a couple of nearly 1,000-foot climbs. In mid-afternoon, it started to rain and continued for about 45 minutes. My clothes were completely soaked, but thankfully my gear remained dry. The cover for my backpack was doing its job. After a 21-mile hike, we reached the Upper Goose Pond Cabin (1,483 ft.) at 5:30. It is a two-story structure, which can accommodate 20 hikers. The cabin is free to thru-hikers, but donations are accepted. The person in charge was a volunteer caretaker named Bonnie. It was packed with hikers along with several of Bonnie's out-of-state friends. Both Pilgrim and I were fortunate to secure a lower bunk for the night.

Day 110—Saturday, July 9, 2011

At breakfast, Bonnie prepared coffee and delicious blueberry pancakes for everyone at the cabin. Pilgrim and I started hiking at 7:30 on a damp morning. It was a difficult day because of tree roots and a great deal of mud caused by rain the day before. There were many boardwalks over muddy areas, but there needed to be many, many more. Mud completely covered the laces of my boots.

The good news was that there was not much increase in elevation. After we had hiked 11 miles, we reached Washington Mountain Road. We hiked 500 feet down the road to the home of the "cookie lady." She gives free cookies to hikers who stop at her house. When we knocked on her door, she greeted us with a small basket containing eight oatmeal chocolate chip cookies. We ate lunch at a picnic table in her front yard in the shade of a large tree with a cool breeze blowing. It was a relaxing and delightful lunch. It didn't take much effort for each of us to devour four cookies for dessert.

We had hiked nearly 21 miles by early evening and reached Dalton (population 6,553). We were in the heart of the Berkshires, which encompasses northwestern Connecticut and the highland region of western Massachusetts. We stopped on Main Street at the Sunoco service station, which Rob Bird manages. Rob operates a hostel, "The Bird Cage," out of his home. Thru-hikers can stay there for free.

Rob gave us directions to his home nearby, where he said the door is never locked. He planned to arrive there a little while later after he closed the service station. The only other hiker staying at the Bird Cage was Badger. He was one of a few guys who at times hiked in a kilt. He claimed it was comfortable and cooler than shorts! Badger was an amiable young man from Illinois, but he had graduated from the University of Wisconsin, where the sports teams are known as Badgers. After a shower, the three of us walked a quarter mile to Jacob's Restaurant for dinner. During our absence, Rob did our laundry. After we returned from dinner, Rob drove all of us to a supermarket to resupply.

Day 111—Sunday, July 10, 2011

In the morning, the three of us felt the need to have an easy day, since we had hiked more than 40 miles over the prior two days. After breakfast at the hostel, Rob shuttled us about nine miles north to the trail in Cheshire, Massachusetts. From there we flip-flopped by hiking south to Dalton, so we could spend another night at The Bird Cage.

In the afternoon, we heard the music of an ice cream truck coming down the street. We raced outside to purchase an ice cream novelty item. It was like being a kid again! Yum! In the evening we treated Rob to dinner at the Old Country Buffet in nearby Pittsfield. It was a very good meal and a great way for us to culminate our satisfying stay at The Bird Cage!

Day 112—Monday, July 11, 2011

At 9:00 a.m., Rob drove the three of us back to the trail at Cheshire to resume our hike heading north. Once we began hiking, Badger picked up his pace and was soon out of sight. It was a tough day of hiking with high humidity and the temperature pushing 90 degrees. It was a difficult 2,500+ foot climb to the top of Mt. Greylock (3,492 ft.), the highest mountain in Massachusetts. Pilgrim and I had lunch at the Bascom Lodge, which is at the summit of the mountain. Then I climbed to the top of the 92-foot stone tower on the mountain and had a spectacular view of a large area including the Green, Catskill, and Taconic Mountains.

In late afternoon, we reached MA 2 at North Adams and walked down the road a half mile to a supermarket. I ate a couple of donuts and drank a pint of chocolate milk. At that point, Pilgrim had a much higher level of energy than I did. When we resumed hiking, he went at a faster pace to reach the Sherman Brook Primitive Campsite (1,300 ft.). As I got near camp, I saw a small sign just off the trail marking Pete's Spring. The water was ice cold, didn't need to be treated, and was truly refreshing. I drank many ounces before filling my Camelbak. Days later we were still talking about the invigorating water of the spring. When I reached the camp, Pilgrim had already set up his tent on a platform. I set up mine next to his, but it barely fit. I had hiked over 16 miles in high heat and humidity.

Day 113—Tuesday, July 12, 2011—Week 17

As we got out of our tents in the early morning, we were shocked to find that two thru-hikers (Wakarusa and Bald Eagle) that were camped right next to us had vanished. We marveled that they could break camp so early and so quietly. We had not heard them, even though they were only about 30 feet away. The sun was out at 6:30 as our trek resumed. In the first few miles of hiking, we had an ascent of more than 1,000 feet.

VERMONT

I saw a sign welcoming me to Vermont and the Long Trail at 8:00 a.m. It was exciting to have completed hiking in 11 states (GA, NC, TN, VA, WV, MD, PA, NJ, NY, CT and MA) with only three states to go. At the border, the AT joins the Long Trail for 105 miles. Then near Killington, the AT separates from the Long Trail and heads northeast toward Maine. The Long Trail continues straight north to the Canadian border for another 168 miles. When the Long Trail was completed in 1930, it became America's first long-distance hiking trail and served as the inspiration for the creation of the AT.

Vermont is a beautiful state, but hiking there is not easy due to rocks, roots, and many miles of bogs. After a heavy rain, walking on the bogs is like walking in soupy mud. It is difficult to keep a positive outlook when facing what seems like an endless muddy trail. During the day, I fell twice. One fall was due to slippery mud, and the other was because of a slick rock. Although I didn't get hurt either time, wallowing in the mud is depressing.

In the late afternoon, there was a 1,000-foot rocky descent and then immediately a 1,000-foot climb. After a day of rather steep ascents and descents covering 18 miles, I was relieved to reach the Melville Nauheim Shelter (2,330 ft.) at 5:45 and set up camp for the night.

Day 114—Wednesday, July 13, 2011

In the morning, it was cool and cloudy. It was an easier day of hiking due to the lower temperature and only moderate climbs. Although there were still plenty of rocks and mud, the biggest problem of the day was tree roots. After hiking over 17 miles, Pilgrim and I reached the Story Spring Shelter (2,810 ft.) at 4:45. We quickly found two places to set up our tents near Wakarusa and Bald Eagle, who had arrived ahead of us. As we began to set up camp, we heard thunder. We hurried to complete setting up our tents before rushing to get water out of the nearby spring. We just made it back to our tents before the rain started about 5:00. It was a close call! The rain continued intermittently overnight.

Day 115—Thursday, July 14, 2011

As we exited our wet tents in the morning, we found that Wakarusa and Bald Eagle had performed their usual and now expected vanishing act! Due to the overnight rain, we got a later start than usual at 7:15. There was a significant climb of 1,700 feet in the late morning to reach the summit of Stratton Mountain (3,936 ft.). Before we ate lunch there, we hung some things out to dry in the sun on the railing of the fire tower.

After lunch, we started a 1,800-foot descent. During the day, we expected more wet bogs and mud due to the rain overnight. However, the trail was surprisingly no worse than the days before. Pilgrim slipped on a wet rock and fell, injuring his wrist. It was bruised and sore. After hiking over 18 miles, we reached the Spruce Peak Shelter (2,180 ft.). We expected to set up camp in the vicinity of the shelter. Due to the rocky and uneven ground, there was absolutely no place to set up a tent. We stayed in the shelter instead.

Day 116—Friday, July 15, 2011

We were looking forward to staying at the Green Mountain House Hostel in Manchester Center, which many hikers had spoken very highly of it. We hiked three miles to VT 11 & 30, arriving at 8:45. The owner of the hostel (Jeff Taussig) was dropping off hikers there that had spent the night at the hostel.

Jeff drove us to downtown Manchester Center, where we went to a restaurant for breakfast. Then we walked to an outfitter called The Mountain Goat, so Pilgrim could buy hiking boots. One of his boots had split on the top, and his attempt to glue it together had failed. I bought new Leki hiking sticks. My old sticks, which I had bought in Georgia, had worn out. I had replaced the tips in Delaware Water Gap, but they had broken off again. Following lunch in town, Pilgrim and I walked to the Price Chopper Supermarket to resupply. Then we called Jeff to pick us up.

When we arrived at the hostel, we realized why it had such a good reputation. The beautiful two-story structure opened for business as a hostel in 2008. We shared a large carpeted bedroom and attached bathroom with Wakarusa and Bald Eagle. Each of us had our own bed with a pillow, fresh linens, and towels. The hostel also offered a fully-equipped kitchen, washer and dryer, television, high-speed internet access, and a free pint of Ben and Jerry's ice cream. What more could a hiker want?

At 6:00 Jeff drove Pilgrim, Wakarusa, Bald Eagle, and me to a restaurant in town. After dinner, we called Jeff. He picked us up and drove us back to the hostel. It was a good day.

Day 117—Saturday, July 16, 2011

Jeff drove many hikers back to the trail in the morning. Pilgrim and I started hiking at 7:20 on a gorgeous day. We had climbs of 1,400 and 1,000 feet. We went up a fire tower at Bromley Mountain (3,260 ft.) for a five-state view. After lunch at the Peru Peak Shelter (2,605 ft.), we crossed wetlands on boardwalks for quite a while. In a few places, the boardwalk was slightly under water. I carefully maneuvered over those areas and somehow managed to keep the inside of my boots dry, which was no easy task!

In the late afternoon, Pilgrim stumbled on a tree root and crashed into a rock. It stunned him, and his face expressed fear of a serious injury. He did have a cut on his forehead but otherwise was OK. After hiking about 15 miles, we reached the Lost Pond Campsite (2,150 ft.) at 3:45. We set up our tents, laid our wet things in the sun to dry, and took a nap for an hour before supper.

Day 118—Sunday, July 17, 2011

We began hiking at 6:40 on a very comfortable day. Pilgrim stumbled again on a rocky descent, but his backpack took the brunt of the fall. Although I did not keep a count of the number of times we each fell, I am sure that he fell many more times than I did. I believe that his falls were mostly related to being in the lead position and constantly looking for white blazes. As a result, I believe he was less cautious in where he stepped.

We ate lunch at the Greenwall Shelter (2,025 ft.). We had climbs of 500, 600, and 1,000 feet during the day. After hiking 15 miles, we reached the Minerva Hinckley Shelter (1,605 ft.) at 3:30. After we set up our tents and secured water, it was only 4:30, so we took a nap for an hour. It began to rain in the later evening and continued for much of the night.

Day 119—Monday, July 18, 2011

The rain had stopped by morning. We left camp at 7:20 and hiked about three miles to where the trail meets VT 103. Pilgrim had arranged for us to meet Sue Brown there. We walked into the parking lot about the same time that Sue arrived. Sue and her husband (Kim), as well as Pilgrim, live in Greenville, South Carolina. Pilgrim knew Sue from her involvement with the local hiking group.

Our first stop was at a supermarket to resupply. Then we stopped at a local ice cream store, where Sue treated us to an ice cream cone. By mid-morning, we arrived at the Browns' lovely summer home on the shore of Lake George in the Adirondacks of New York State. Pilgrim and I put our tents outside to dry, did laundry, had lunch, and took a nap.

In the late afternoon, we went down to the dock, and Kim drove us all around the lake in a power boat. During the voyage, Sue told the history of many of the properties and related interesting stories about some of the owners. When we got back, I took a brief swim in the cool water. In the evening, Kim grilled steak for dinner. We sat at a picnic table in the back yard, enjoying a wonderful meal, interesting conversation, and a spectacular view of the lake. What a relaxing and fun day!

Day 120—Tuesday, July 19, 2011—Week 18

In the early morning, the Browns drove us about 45 minutes back to the trail in Vermont. We said goodbye and thanked them for their warm hospitality. We began hiking shortly before 8:00. A highlight of the day was seeing a sign indicating that we were just 500 miles from Mt. Katahdin. After hiking over 1,700 miles, that distance didn't seem so far. However, I knew that the hardest part of the trail was still ahead. Right next to the mileage sign was a cooler with sodas. It was obvious that trail magic was left at that exact place to encourage hikers to celebrate their achievement.

The most difficult part of the day involved a 2,500-foot climb over endless rocks and roots. Near the end of the day, the AT split from the Long Trail. After hiking over 18 miles, we reached the Tucker-Johnson Shelter/ Campsite (2,300 ft.) and set up camp. The shelter was no longer in existence, but there was a level place to set up our tents. We were the only hikers there for the night.

Day 121—Wednesday, July 20, 2011

We began hiking just before 7:00. We reached the Gifford Woods State Park in Killington by mid-morning. As we were exiting the park and crossing the road, we heard someone shout "Buckeye." I turned and saw Nachita and Poncho, whom I had first met at the Bears Den Hostel in Virginia. Then I had seen them again in Pennsylvania. They had spent a day with a friend and were returning to hike the trail.

A little while later, we reached Thundering Falls, a waterfall that has a drop of 125 feet. It is a beautiful site and displays nature at its best. Next we climbed over Quimby Mountain (2,640 ft.), before stopping for lunch at the Stony Brook Shelter (1,380 ft.). There was a young hiker at the shelter who seemed to be just taking it easy. When Pilgrim asked him where he was headed he said, "I'm heading south, but I don't know how far I'll go." I thought how different his hike was from mine. Every night I knew how far I had hiked that day, and how far I planned to go the next day!

In the afternoon, the weather got warm, and I was running low on water. After we crossed a road, I saw a house just a short distance away. I went to the house and knocked on the front door. No one answered. Then I walked around the house and knocked on the back door. No one answered. I intended to ask if I could take some water out of the hose. I decided that there would be no harm done if I simply took a few liters of water. I reasoned that if a hiker stopped at my house and found no one home, I wouldn't mind if he took a few liters of water.

After I had filled my Camelbak, I made sure that the hose was turned off. I thanked the home owners, even though they could not hear me. About 6:00 we reached Winturri Shelter (1,910 ft.) and set up camp. We had hiked 19 miles.

Day 122—Thursday, July 21, 2011

It was good to get an early start at 6:40 in the morning. During the day, the temperature reached 98 degrees with high humidity. The highest climbs for the day were 600, 700, and 1,000-feet. Pilgrim and I stopped for lunch at a store less than a half mile off the AT. We each bought a bottle of root beer and a pint of vanilla ice cream and made a root-beer float to go along with our sandwiches. We ate lunch at a picnic table in the shade of a large tree. Amazingly, there was a breeze, which along with the ice cream and soda, actually chilled my body in the heat of the day. It was the only time during the day that I felt cool.

After lunch, I called Joe Stagliano, the brother of a friend, Dick Stagliano. Joe agreed to pick Pilgrim and me up about 4:00 at the country store on VT 14 in West Hartford, Vermont. We arrived a little later than we had expected. Joe and his wife, Mary, were waiting for us.

We had hiked nearly 17 miles for the day in oppressive heat. After introductions, I showed Joe and Mary how hot I was during the day. I took the chamois cloth I had used to wipe my face and twisted it. I was amazed how much water it held. My sweat made a good-sized puddle on the ground. After Pilgrim and I went into the store and got a cold drink, we returned to the Staglianos' air-conditioned car. They drove us about 20 miles to their beautiful home in New Hampshire, which is on a small lake. In the evening, we showered, did laundry, and enjoyed dinner.

Day 123—Friday, July 22, 2011

After breakfast, Mary drove us about 20 miles back to the trail in Vermont at 6:30. As Pilgrim and I began hiking, we went through a forest. The needles from the trees created a cushion effect and were comfortable to walk on. As the day progressed, the temperature was not nearly as high as the prior day. After a ten-mile hike, we crossed a bridge over the Connecticut River, which marks the Vermont/New Hampshire border.

NEW HAMPSHIRE

I had completed hiking in 12 states on the trail (GA, NC, TN, VA, WV, MD, PA, NJ, NY, CT, MA and VT), as I entered New Hampshire. Twelve states down, two states to go. New Hampshire and Maine are considered the two most difficult states to hike on the entire AT. In a sense, these two states are in a class above the rest. I thought of the adage of saving the best for last. More appropriately, the AT had saved the toughest for last. Then I thought of how southbound thru-hikers take on Maine and New Hampshire first. I was glad to have worked up to hiking in those states, rather than starting with them.

We continued hiking into the downtown of Hanover (population 8,636), the home of Dartmouth College. The upscale town has many shops in a thriving downtown business district. I went to the Post Office, where I sent home my lighter-weight clothes and picked up warmer ones for hiking at higher elevations in the northeast. Pilgrim and I had lunch at Subway, visited two outfitters, and used the computer at the public library.

Amy Vanderkooi, the daughter of Verna Vanderkooi, a former colleague at Cuyahoga Community College, lives and works near Hanover. She offered to assist me when I reached Hanover. In the late afternoon, she picked up Pilgrim and me at the library and drove us to a supermarket in town, the Hanover Food Co-op. After we resupplied, Amy drove us a few miles out of town to the Sunset Motor Inn. Pilgrim and I were eager to spend the warm night in an air-conditioned room. While we were hiking, we had learned that there was another hiker who was also using the trail name of Pilgrim. We had seen his entries several times in registers at shelters. At the motel, we met the other Pilgrim, who was an ordained minister.

Day 124—Saturday, July 23, 2011

A taxi arrived at the motel at 6:30 in the morning to drive us about three miles back to the trail. We were able to begin hiking about ten minutes later. We had climbs during the day of 700 feet, 900 feet, and two at 1,000 feet. Our major concern was availability of water, as several sources were dry. Once again, the weather was hot with the temperature hitting 90 degrees. Our highest elevation of the day was at the South Peak of Moose Mountain (2,290 ft.). We had lunch at the Moose Mountain Shelter (1,850 ft.). After lunch, we rested for about an hour. We reached the Trapper John Shelter (1,345 ft.) at 6:15 and set up camp. We hiked about 17 miles.

I knew many hikers staying in or around the shelter. One hiker, whom I met for the first time, was Dead Man. I had seen his name in the trail registers and heard about him from the man who drove me to resupply in Port Clinton, Pennsylvania. Dead Man told me that he got his trail name after hiking in cold, wet weather in early March. When he arrived at the hostel at Neels Gap, GA, he was shaking and hypothermic. Blankets were placed over him for warmth. The operator of the hostel said to hikers, "I think we have a dead man in there!" The next day Dead Man, whose real name is Terry O'Brien, was driven home to Roswell, Georgia. Within several days, he had recovered and was back on the trail!

Day 125—Sunday, July 24, 2011

Pilgrim and I started hiking at 6:45. It was great day weather wise, cooler and less humid. Our main concern again was the shortage of water. At the start of a normal day of hiking, I usually carried about two liters of water. Because of the extremely hot weather, I decided to carry about three liters. Since a liter of water weighs about two pounds, that meant carrying about two extra pounds on my back.

In the late morning, we reached the highest elevation point of the day at the abandoned fire tower on Smarts Mountain (3,230 ft.). We climbed the tower to get a panoramic view of the area. During the extensive day of climbing, we had ascents of 800 feet, 1,500 feet, and 2,400 feet. After hiking 19 miles over nearly 12 hours, we reached the Ore Hill Shelter (1,720 ft.) at 6:30. We set up camp and were pleased to find a spring on the path 100 yards in front of the shelter.

Day 126—Monday, July 25, 2011

We began our hike at 6:45. In mid-morning, we reached NH 25, considered to be a southern boundary of the White Mountains. When we arrived at the Jeffers Brook Shelter (1,350 ft.) in the late morning, we decided to eat an early lunch. We heard that a possible thunderstorm could hit in the early afternoon. Mt. Moosilauke (4,802 ft.) was less than five miles ahead. It is the first place on the AT that is above tree line. We needed to climb about 3,500 feet to reach its summit. We were slowed as Pilgrim pulled a thigh muscle going up the mountain. The ascent took three hours over steep and rocky terrain. During that time we took only two five-minute breaks. As we approached the top, the weather got nastier. A misty rain fell, and it got much colder.

The wind was blowing at about 30 mph on the summit, and no other hikers were anywhere in sight. I felt as if I were hiking in a cold foggy wind tunnel. Visibility was very limited, and my eyes watered. Gusts of cold wind blew me from side to side, on and off the trail. I was perturbed when I heard a voice say, "Please stay on the trail!" I squinted and saw a ridge runner whose job involved protecting the fragile alpine vegetation. He had on a winter parka, gloves and a hat, and was protected from the wind by a large rock. I replied in an agitated voice, "I'm trying, but it is very difficult to see where I am going."

After about 15 minutes of fighting the severe weather conditions on the summit, we began to descend on the north side of the mountain about 3:00. Soon we were protected by small pine trees on each side of the narrow trail, which buffeted us from the wind. Although I thought the worst was over, going down the mountain about 3,000 feet was much more demanding than going up. The misty rain made every rock a potential hazard. Several places on the steep trail there were wooden blocks imbedded in rock to offer safer footing, hand bars to grip, and wooden step ladders to descend from extreme heights to lower levels. Pilgrim fell twice going down the mountain, and he had swelling on his arm and leg. I tried to keep Pilgrim's spirits up as I understood that he was hurting. I told him how difficult the trail was, and how he was not slowing me down much at all. What I said was true! Although I felt fine, I slipped and nearly fell several times. Even in good weather, it would have been a slow dangerous descent.

We reached NH 112 at Kinsman Notch about 6:30 and called for a shuttle. We were driven about five miles to the One Step at a Time Hostel in Lincoln. About 20 hikers were staying there. Since there were only six bunks and a couch, most slept on the garage floor as I did. Pilgrim was able to secure the couch. We had hiked 17 miles during the difficult 12-hour day. The good news was that Mt. Katahdin was now less than 400 miles ahead.

Day 127—Tuesday, July 26, 2011—Week 19

We took a zero day, giving Pilgrim a day of recovery. It was my first day of total rest since my family had visited me about 50 days before in Harpers Ferry. Pilgrim and I walked to a pancake restaurant for breakfast. Next we stopped at a medical clinic, where he was able to make an afternoon appointment to see a physician's assistant for his sore leg. Then we resupplied at a supermarket and returned to the hostel to do our laundry.

About noon, the parents of a thru-hiker (Orange Blaze) arrived at the hostel to visit their son and to provide trail magic. They brought plenty of food and drink to share with all the hikers. I had met Orange Blaze in Tennessee in April. However, I had not seen him since then. It was great to reminisce about our adventure. Orange Blaze told me the bad news that Lost had suffered a knee injury and was unable to continue his hike. I had hiked many days with Lost. Since he had previously thru-hiked the Pacific Crest and Continental Divide trails, I just expected him to be successful in completing the AT. Once again, I was reminded that injury could hit anyone at any time on the trail and end the dream of a successful thru-hike.

In mid-afternoon, Pilgrim went to the clinic, and I went to the library to use the computer. When Pilgrim returned from his medical appointment, he reported that his injuries were diagnosed as merely muscular. He was told to use an over-the-counter medication as needed for soreness. In the evening, Pilgrim and I walked downtown for pizza. He paid the bill in appreciation of my understanding and encouragement of him in dealing with his injury on Mount Moosilauke.

Day 128—Wednesday, July 27, 2011

In the early morning, a shuttle picked us up at the hostel. After a 15-minute ride back to Kinsman Notch in the White Mountains, we resumed hiking at 7:00. We had a 1,600-foot rocky and steep climb over the East Peak of Mount Wolf (3,478 ft.). During the late morning, I bruised my left hand preventing a fall while on a descent. It ached a little, but it was not serious.

We stopped along the trail and ate lunch at 12:30. Then we hiked for about an hour before we reached the Eliza Brooks Shelter (2,400 ft.). It was mid-afternoon, and we decided to take a rest. Although we had hiked less than eight miles, we remained at the shelter. Pilgrim's leg was still bothering him. He did not want to continue hiking since we were about to face an ascent of about 2,000 feet over the very difficult Kinsman Mountains. We set up our tents for the night. We must have been tired as we napped for over two hours before eating dinner.

Day 129—Thursday, July 28, 2011

It was once again a cool day in the White Mountains. We knew that it was a tough climb to scale the Kinsman Mountains. We had to rock scramble and use our hands many times. We finally reached the summit of South Kinsman Mountain (4,358 ft.) by 10:30. We passed Dead Man on the ascent and spoke about how we worried that a potentially tragic fall could end our hike.

Within an hour after that conversation, a disastrous event occurred. As I was making a steep descent on a smooth, large, flat rock, my feet went out from underneath me. As I fell, my right leg went under my body. Upon landing, I let out an anguished cry. I knew immediately that I had injured my ankle severely. I thought of why I had fallen. My boots had little tread on the soles, and I had taken too long a stride instead of shuffling my feet on the smooth sloping rock. As I lay resting on the rock for several minutes, I thought that my attempt to thru-hike the AT might end because of the fall I had just taken.

A few minutes later, Dead Man caught up with us. He offered to carry my pack, but I refused. I told him to continue hiking. About five minutes later, I stood up and began to hobble ahead. As I inched forward on the trail, Dead Man reappeared. He had reached the Kinsman Pond Shelter/Campsite (3,750 ft.), and he returned to tell us that it was just a short distance ahead. He had left his backpack at the campsite. When Dead Man again offered to carry my pack, I agreed. The short hike to the shelter/campsite took several minutes. I was very afraid of falling again on the treacherous terrain. Thankfully, I made it to the shelter/campsite safely. I was greeted by a caretaker (Stephanie), who gave me a bag of a dry chemical. When it was crushed, it felt like an ice pack. I applied it to my ankle until the bag no longer felt cold. Then Stephanie wrapped my ankle with an ace bandage.

The cost to stay at a shelter or campsite in the White Mountains is $8/person per night. Stephanie said that Pilgrim and I could set up our tents on a nearby tent platform, which could accommodate two tents. After putting up my tent, I elevated my ankle, resting it on the top of my backpack. When I was off my feet, the ankle did not hurt. In the afternoon and evening, Pilgrim encouraged me to plan to hike the next day. I didn't see how that was possible. My night's sleep was interrupted several times, as I turned in my tent. I discovered that the best position to prevent pain was to sleep on my back.

Day 130—Friday, July 29, 2011

In the morning, my ankle was moderately swollen. Pilgrim pleaded again with me to continue hiking, even if I went at a very slow pace. I told him that I was not able to hike, even on level ground, let alone hike in the White Mountains. He finally realized that I would not resume hiking for at least several days. He was very disappointed with my decision.

I thought of how I could best deal with my injury. I needed to get advice from an orthopedic doctor. Then I thought of Dr. Kim Brown, a retired orthopedic surgeon, whom I had met less than two weeks ago. Pilgrim and I had spent a wonderful day with Sue and Kim in Lake George, New York, on July 18. I asked Pilgrim for the Browns' telephone number. At that point it was still too early in the morning to call. I suggested that Pilgrim resume hiking, and hopefully I would be able to catch up with him later on the trail. Before he resumed hiking about 8:00, he said a lengthy prayer, asking God to heal my ankle and reunite us on the trail. I was emotionally moved as I wondered if I would be able to resume hiking at all or if I would see him again.

About 9:00 I spoke with Dr. Brown. He asked me several questions about the fall and how the ankle felt. He said that only an x-ray could determine whether the ankle was broken or just severely sprained. He recommended that I walk on a flat surface, like the tent platform, for several minutes at a time to evaluate the condition of the ankle and to initiate the healing process. He advised that I should not take an anti-inflammatory drug, like Ibuprofen, unless the ankle caused me pain. Finally, he suggested that I purchase an Aircast Air-Stirrup ankle brace, which would stabilize and minimize side-to-side movement of the ankle. The ankle brace would provide support, and the graduated compression it offered would help reduce edema, the swelling caused by fluids trapped in the tissue around the ankle. The problem was where to buy it and how to get it while I was immobilized and confined on the mountain.

I had another problem too. My cell phone was nearly out of power, so Dr. Brown offered to call my wife and explain what had happened. Perhaps Nancy could arrange somehow for me to get the ankle brace. When I eventually spoke with her, she had failed to find any business with an ankle brace in stock.

In desperation, I called my daughter, Michelle. I asked her to check on the computer what drugstores were in Lincoln, the closest town to where I was. She found a phone number for a Rite-Aid Pharmacy. I called the store and was told that there was one ankle brace in stock. I paid $40 for it with a credit card and explained my situation. I said that the device could be given to anyone who came into the store asking for it in my name. Then I called Chet West, owner of the One Step at a Time Hostel in Lincoln, where I had stayed just a few nights before. Chet said he would have a hiker go to Rite-Aid, get the ankle brace, and bring it up to me. The fantastic news gave me joy and hope.

Several times during the day, I got out of my tent and walked for five-to-ten minutes on the wooden platform as Dr. Brown had suggested. Since Pilgrim's tent was gone, there was a small open area. To avoid the monotony of simply walking back and forth, I tried to be creative. I walked to form various shapes including a triangle, rectangle, circle, and cross. I never got off the platform, because the terrain around it was rocky and uneven.

About 5:00 I heard someone call out loudly, "Buckeye Flash!" I responded, "I'm over here." I was surprised to see two hikers. One hiker said, "We have something for you." He handed me the ankle brace. I thanked both hikers and gave each $10 for their time and trouble. Then I asked, "Where are you headed tonight?" I assumed that they were southbound hikers and would continue hiking in that direction. One hiker responded, "We're headed back to Chet's." "Why are you going back there?" I asked. "We're waiting for a friend to catch up with us!" one hiker replied. These two hikers had climbed a very difficult mountain for me and were now returning to where they started. I was very impressed by their effort on my behalf. I said, "Wow, I would like to give each of you another $10 for your help." "No, give it to Chet!" each of the hikers replied. Chet West does not charge a fee for a hiker to stay at his hostel, but he does accept donations. I agreed to the hikers' request that the additional money would be donated to Chet.

Before they left, one hiker said to me, "Do you need anything else?" I responded, "I am about out of any bread product like bagels." One hiker said, "We'll see about getting you some bagels tomorrow." "That would be great," I replied. I was thankful for the hikers' help and wished them well. Just as they turned to leave, a light rain began to fall. After they left, I read the instructions for the ankle brace. Since it was raining lightly and soon to be dark, I decided to wait until morning to begin using my new device. It continued to rain lightly overnight.

Day 131—Saturday, July 30, 2011

The rain had stopped by morning, but it was damp, windy, and cool. I was eager to put on the ankle brace and test it. It was somewhat difficult to get my right foot into my boot while I was wearing the ankle brace. I had to unloosen the laces on my boot completely and put my foot gingerly into it. When I first walked with the ankle brace, I was encouraged. It definitely supported the ankle and prevented side-to-side movement. During the day, I walked on the platform wearing the ankle brace many times, adding up to about 30 minutes.

In the afternoon, I heard someone call my name. It was a new lone hiker delivering a six-pack of bagels. It was great to have the bagels to eat with my peanut butter and cheese. Once again, I gave the hiker $10 for his effort. He also was a southbound hiker, and he too was headed back to Chet's in Lincoln.

Because of that, I offered him another $10. Like the other hikers, he said, "Give it to Chet." I agreed to do that. I was so impressed by the help that I got from the hiking community. I felt proud to be a part of such a supportive group.

In early evening, Stephanie checked on how I was doing. I told her that I wanted to resume hiking the next morning, and I hoped to reach Chet's hostel in Lincoln. She offered to carry my backpack to the Lonesome Lake Hut, the southernmost hut in the White Mountains. It was just two miles ahead on the dangerous trail. Stephanie said that the assistant manager of the Lonesome Lake Hut (Luke) would carry my backpack the rest of the way down North Kinsman Mountain to the general store at Franconia Notch. I was pleased to accept the help.

The Appalachian Mountain Club (AMC) operates eight huts in the White Mountains over a 63-mile area. They are fully-enclosed lodges and sleep 36-90 people. Although rates vary depending on the hut and day of the week, an overnight's stay can cost upwards of $100/person. The cost includes dinner, breakfast, bunk space, pillow, and blanket. Some people hike from hut to hut during the summer season. Each hut has a manager and staff during the full-service summer season.

Day 132—Sunday, July 31, 2011

After more than two days of being at the campsite, I needed to get off the mountain. I left at 6:15 on a dry day, and it felt good to be hiking again. I moved very, very slowly as my right ankle was extremely tender. As I navigated over rocks and steep descents, I felt some pain at times. The terrain was brutal, but I was determined to remain upright. I estimated that I was hiking at about 1/3 or less of my normal pace.

Stephanie began hiking about 7:30, carrying my backpack. She caught up with me about 8:00. The distance that I had hiked in one hour and 45 minutes, took her about 30 minutes. By 9:00 we reached the Lonesome Lake Hut. The area around the hut is beautiful. I wished that I could have sat down and taken some time to enjoy the view.

As promised, Luke began to carry my backpack about three miles down the mountain. He was soon out of my sight as I struggled and inched ahead. Thankfully, the trail seemed to get easier the farther down the mountain I went. I wondered why I saw so many people on the trail heading south toward the hut. Very few people carried even a small backpack. Then I remembered it was the weekend when many people go for a day hike.

About 1:00 I walked into the store at the foot of the mountain and reclaimed my backpack. It had taken me almost seven hours to hike about five miles. I called for a shuttle to take me to the hostel in Lincoln. I met the driver at the nearby parking lot on U.S. 3. Unfortunately, it cost me $20 because I was the only passenger. Had there been four hikers to share the cost, I would have paid only $5.

When I reached the hostel about 1:30, I thanked Chet for his help and told him I would be sending him a check for $50 when I got home. I explained that $30 of the $50 was donated by the three hikers who visited me on the mountain and brought me the ankle brace and bagels. The remaining $20 was a token of my appreciation for coordinating the "rescue process."

Just after I arrived at the hostel, a young man (Jason) with cerebral palsy was walking by on the road in front of the hostel. Chet saw him and greeted him with a smile. I overheard much of their conversation. Jason was elated by Chet's positive and supportive remarks. The whole experience of seeing Chet interact with Jason impressed me. It further convinced me of what a good man Chet West is.

I borrowed a bike that Chet had hanging in his garage to go to a pizza shop to eat supper. Then I pedaled to a supermarket to resupply. The bicycle saved me from walking at least two miles on the injured ankle.

Chet told me that Pilgrim and Dead Man had stayed at the hostel two nights earlier and were hiking together. I was exactly two days behind them, and I knew my pace would be much slower than theirs. Therefore, I reasoned that the only way I could possibly catch up with them was to hike longer each day than they would. In the evening, I arranged for a shuttle to pick me up at 6:00 the next morning to drive me back to the trail.

Day 133—Monday, August 1, 2011

The shuttle finally arrived at nearly 7:00. I let the driver know that I was upset as I had been waiting since 6:00. I was driven back to Franconia Notch (1,450 ft.) and began hiking at 7:15. My ankle felt about the same as it had the day before. I hiked slowly as it was very tender and weak. Although rain was in the forecast, thankfully the weather was good. During most of the beautiful day, I was on the awesome Franconia Ridge. I thought of how much tougher hiking on the ridge would have been in inclement weather.

In the White Mountains, the AT is commonly referred to on signs by the name of the local trail it follows, e.g., Franconia Ridge Trail. I climbed over 3,400 feet to reach Little Haystack (4,800 ft.) and had lunch sitting on a rock at the summit. There were spectacular vistas in all directions. Then I climbed over Mt. Lincoln (5,089 ft.) followed by Mt. Lafayette (5,260 ft.). I hiked about three more miles to reach Garfield Pond (3,860 ft.). I found a stealth campsite about 25 feet from the shore. It was 7:45 as I set up my tent.

I had hiked slightly more than nine miles in over 12 hours. I was satisfied as I had passed my first full-day test of hiking after the serious ankle injury. I had dealt successfully with the rugged and rocky terrain coupled with the high ascents and descents. When I went to sleep, I did not take off the ankle brace. It provided stability when I moved from side to side, and my sleep was less interrupted too.

A cairn marks the trail on Franconia Ridge, NH

Day 134—Tuesday, August 2, 2011—Week 20

I was awake about 5:30 in the morning. After I took down my tent, I looked out at Garfield Pond and saw the beautiful reflection of the surrounding trees. As I began hiking before 7:00, I immediately faced a rock scramble up rugged Mt. Garfield (4,500 ft.). The ascent was only 640 feet, but it was quite difficult. I had to use my arm strength to pull my body up and over large rocks. At times I looked at where I needed to go and wondered whether I could get there. Somehow my determination and arm strength made it happen!

When I reached the top of Mt. Garfield, I faced a new challenge. I began a 700-foot descent over a large rock pile on my way to the Galehead Hut (3,800 ft.). I stopped on the descent and called Cindi. I told her where I was and wished she could see what I was facing.

During the whole day, it was very slow going as I was nervous dealing with the rough terrain.

When I reached the Galehead Hut, it was time for lunch. I enjoyed a few bowls of soup and a slice of pumpkin bread. The huts have a reputation for good food, and my expectations were met. As I resumed hiking, it started to drizzle,

The steep and rugged descent of Mt. Garfield, NH

and the temperature began to drop. I put on my rain jacket. I faced a climb of over 1,000 feet up the South Twin Mountain (4,902 ft.), before descending to Mt. Guyot (4,580 ft.).

A young couple who were section hikers caught up with me. We talked for several minutes as we hiked. Then I slipped and fell, and I let out a scream! My ankle hurt, and I was scared that I may have caused more severe injury to it. It was the first time I had fallen since I was on North Kinsman Mountain five days before. The couple stopped and expressed their concern. As the pain diminished, I resumed hiking slowly. I told the couple that I was all right and urged them to continue at their own pace. They said goodbye and soon were out of sight.

Within 30 minutes, the rain picked up. It was early evening, and I was still over three miles from the next hut and about eight miles from the next shelter/campsite. I kept surveying the landscape for a good place to stealth camp, but the ground was uneven and small trees seemed to be everywhere. It took me about 15 minutes to spot a tiny and very marginal site about 25 feet off the trail. I could barely get my tent set up in the space available, but at least the ground was reasonably level. I worked feverishly to get the tent up quickly as a light rain fell.

By the time I was done putting up the rain fly, the floor of the tent was wet. I took my chamois cloth and tried to dry it the best I could. Then I started to shake slightly. I sensed that I was getting close to being hypothermic. I immediately put on dry clothes and got into my sleeping bag. Within about ten minutes, I was no longer shaking. I ate an energy bar for my supper. I had hiked only eight miles, but it was the best I could do under the trying circumstances.

Day 135—Wednesday, August 3, 2011

By morning, the rain had stopped, but it was replaced by a light fog. It was slow going as I took down the wet tent and packed my damp belongings. I put the same wet clothes back on that I had taken off the prior night. Although putting on wet clothes may seem very difficult, I got quite used to it. Usually it took me only a few minutes, and I forgot that the clothes were even wet. I started hiking at 7:30. During the morning, there was some rock scrambling.

When I reached the Zealand Falls Hut (2,630 ft.), I enjoyed a couple of bowls of delicious and inexpensive soup. After I left the hut, the trail became much less rocky, and it was a welcome turn of events. The trail went through wetlands for a few miles. Not surprisingly, I found that walking on boards over wetlands was much easier than rock scrambling. By late afternoon, I reached the Saco River (1,277 ft.). I lost about a half hour trying to find a white blaze that marked the trail. Once I found the trail again, soon I was climbing the steep Webster Cliffs (3,350 ft.). As darkness was near, I began to look for a location to set up my tent. I spotted a small level spot just off the trail. It was barely large enough to set up my tent. I had hiked 11 miles, the farthest since I had injured my ankle.

Day 136—Thursday, August 4, 2011

I began hiking at 6:30 on a nice day. Within ten minutes, I came upon a free campsite with several good places to set up a tent. The campsite was not mentioned in the *Appalachian Trail Thru-Hiker's Companion*. Had I known that it existed, I would have passed on the small site I used the night before. After I got over Webster Cliffs, I climbed Mt. Webster (3,910 ft.). In less than two miles, I was over Mt. Jackson (4,052 ft.). Then I stopped for an early lunch at the Mizpah Spring Hut (3,800 ft.). I was getting quite used to eating delicious soup at nearly every hut in the White Mountains. After lunch, I climbed Mt. Clinton (4,312 ft.), which was formerly Mt. Pierce. The last mountain I climbed was Mt. Franklin (5,004 ft.).

After hiking 10 miles, I reached the Lake of the Clouds Hut (5,050 ft.) about 4:00. It is the largest and most popular of the eight huts in the White Mountains. The reason is because it is near Mt. Washington (6,299 ft.), the highest peak in the Northeast.

My feet were tender from the rocky terrain, but I felt that my ankle was slowly improving each day. I was able to hike slightly faster than I had just a few

Lake of the Clouds Hut near Mt. Washington, NH

days before. However, during each day my foot would often hit a rock, and the resulting pain would remind me that the ankle was far from healed.

When I arrived at the Lake of the Clouds Hut, I sought a work-for-stay exchange. This option is available at each hut to between two and four thru-hikers each night on a first-come, first-serve basis. In exchange for light work, a thru-hiker gets to sleep on the floor of the hut. After the paying guests have finished eating a delicious dinner and breakfast, the hiker can eat the leftovers for free. Most thru-hikers hope to be offered this opportunity. I soon discovered that there were two hikers who had arrived ahead of me at the Lake of the Clouds Hut, and they both had taken advantage of the work plan.

It was my first night at a hut in the White Mountains, and I was pleased to be the third hiker to accept the work plan. My job was to wipe off the ten dining room tables before and after the guests ate. I also had to wash dishes after dinner. Within an hour of my arrival, many other hikers reached the hut. They were not offered a work-for-stay exchange. Instead they paid $15 to stay in the "dungeon" below the hut. They also got to eat dinner and breakfast after the full-paying guests had eaten. The dungeon was a windowless, small basement shelter that slept six. I was pleased that I did not need to stay in the dungeon as it was a rather depressing place.

After the dungeon was full, two other thru-hikers arrived. They were Arthur Dent and Rain Dance. Surprisingly to me, they each received a work-for-stay exchange as well. I believe the reason was that the weather around the hut can become life threatening in a short time. A surface wind speed of 231 mph was recorded at nearby Mt. Washington in 1934. It stood as the official world record from 1934 until 2010. The staff of the hut did not want to deny hikers a place to stay and turn them out into the elements since there are no other places to stay or camp within many miles. Arthur Dent and Rain Dance were given the job of sweeping the floor after meals and washing and drying dishes as well. Their late arrival actually turned into an advantage over hikers who had arrived earlier and were staying in the dungeon.

Day 137—Friday, August 5, 2011

After breakfast, I wiped the dining-room tables. Then I was out the door and on my way about 8:30. I did not stay for breakfast because I didn't want to take the time it would involve. I felt that I needed to begin hiking to have any chance of eventually catching up with Pilgrim and Dead Man. I had about a 1,300-foot ascent over less than two miles to reach Mt. Washington. It was slow going on the very rocky trail, and it took me until mid-morning to reach the famous summit. Mt. Washington is accessible by hiking trails, car, and the cog railway.

Upon arriving at Mt. Washington, I went to the snack bar and made a purchase. The sun was shining brightly on the warm day. I was well above tree line, and there was no shade. As I watched the Cog Railway go downhill toward the foot of the mountain, I began a slow 2,000-foot descent over four miles on the extremely rocky trail.

In the early afternoon, I spotted a flat rock and used it as a place to sit and enjoy my lunch. The worst part of the hike was that my hiking sticks collapsed over and over as I was trying to use them for balance and support. I kept resetting them to the desired height I wanted. The condition of the hiking sticks really worried me, especially on steep descents. On one occasion, I fell hard because of the faltering sticks. I sat on the rocks until the pain stopped. The fall and subsequent abrasion weakened my spirit. I felt very frustrated and mentally exhausted. I thought that if the rest of the hike went as poorly, I would want to quit.

In the mid-afternoon, the trail ascended about 1,200 feet before finally descending about the same distance to the Madison Spring Hut (4,300 ft.). About 4:30, I reached the hut and found many people outside who were milling around and talking. The Madison Spring Hut was the nicest of all. It looked new, and it had been recently rebuilt. Although I had hiked only slightly more than seven miles, it seemed more like 21 miles.

I entered the hut and asked to speak with the manager. I was not optimistic about getting a work-for-stay exchange as I knew that there were at least two thru-hikers at the hut before me. As I expected, the two hikers I knew had secured the first two work options and were given kitchen duty. To my pleasant surprise, there was still one position available. The hut manager asked me if I would be willing to speak with the paying guests about my thru-hiking adventure. That offer sounded almost too good to be true. Of course, I happily accepted his request. In return for the fun job of sharing my recent experience, I got a very nice place to stay for free with great food! Life was good again! Soon after I had gotten the good news, Arthur Dent and Rain Dance arrived at the hut. They were unable to get a work-for-stay exchange, so they left the hut and continued hiking about two miles to the nearest camping area.

Soon I sat down at one of the dining room tables and began talking with a section hiker and his son. When I told the man about my collapsing hiking sticks, he offered to fix my problem. He used a small screwdriver to tighten the screws and jokingly called himself my hiking stick mechanic. I was grateful for his help! I had no more problems with my hiking sticks the rest of the hike.

The following night I expected to stay at the White Mountains Lodge and Hostel in Shelburne, where I believed that Pilgrim and Dead Man would also be staying. Before I got hurt, Pilgrim had told me that he was going to take a zero day there as his wife was going to visit him. You may wonder how Pilgrim and Dead Man could be two days ahead of me and yet all of us be at the same place the next night. It was because I planned to get a shuttle the next afternoon from Pinkham Notch to the hostel. Although I would be with Pilgrim and Dead Man at the hostel in the evening, I would still be two hiking days or 21 trail miles behind them.

If Pilgrim and Dead Man took a zero day as expected, I would only be one day behind. However, I planned to ask them to take a second zero day, and then I would be able to catch up with them. I called the White Mountains Lodge and Hostel and made a reservation to stay the next evening. Once I reached Pinkham Notch, I planned to call the hostel for a shuttle to pick me up.

I enjoyed a delicious dinner at the Madison Spring Hut. When the other hikers and I told the hut manager that dinner was definitely better than at the Lake of the Clouds Hut, he was all smiles. My presentation about my thru-hike seemed to be well received by the guests at the hut. After I finished my remarks, I answered several questions.

Day 138—Saturday, August 6, 2011

I was the first hiker out the door of the hut at 6:00. I skipped the prepared breakfast once again in order to get a very early start. I would not have been able to start hiking until more than two hours later if I had waited for what was surely a delicious breakfast at the hut. I knew that the eight miles I needed to hike to reach Pinkham Notch would be slow and difficult. The payoff though was that I could spend the night at the hostel in Shelburne.

The trail was tougher than on the horrendous day before. It was really steep, and the rocks were very large and jagged. I climbed about 1,100 feet in a half mile to reach the summit of Mt. Madison (5,366 ft.). Each successful step without a fall was like a small victory. I was moving very slowly, and I had little choice but to do so. I thought that my decision to get an early start was certainly the correct one. By 9:00, one of the thru-hikers who had stayed at the Madison Spring Hut caught up with me. Before he passed me, he commented on the steepness and ruggedness of the trail. A little while later, the other thru-hiker from the hut passed me too. Both of those hikers were young, fit, and uninjured.

From the summit of Mt. Madison, the trail descended over 3,000 feet in a little over three miles to the West Branch of the Peabody River (2,300 ft.). From there the trail began a 560-foot ascent to Low's Bald Spot (2,860 ft.) before descending over 800 feet to the Pinkham Notch Visitor Center (2,050 ft.) at NH 16. It was mid-afternoon when I arrived there and called for a shuttle to the hostel. I celebrated my successful day by buying a snack and soda.

Sitting on the covered porch of the Visitor Center, I waited for the shuttle. In a little while, Arthur Dent and Rain Dance arrived before moving on. After a long wait, the shuttle finally arrived. I reached the hostel about 3:30. It was a clean and beautifully restored 19th century farmhouse in the heart of the White Mountains where NH 2 and the AT intersect.

After I showered, I awaited the arrival of Pilgrim and Dead Man. They appeared about 5:00, looking beat. I surprised them, and they were startled to see me. They had no clue that I would be at the hostel. "How did you get here?" Pilgrim asked. "I got a shuttle from Pinkham Notch," I replied. Pilgrim and Dead Man had stayed at the Joe Dodge Lodge at Pinkham Notch two nights before. As I had expected, they agreed to take a second zero day, so I could catch up. In the early evening, we spoke about our adventurous journey. I told them what had happened since my ankle injury 10 days previously on North Kinsman Mountain.

Day 139—Sunday, August 7, 2011

After breakfast, I was shuttled back to Pinkham Notch to resume hiking at 8:00. It was a dull, damp day with light rain falling. Although the weather was foul, my outlook was positive. I reflected on the fact that after I injured my ankle, Pilgrim and Dead Man had gotten a two-day lead. Since then, the lead had remained the same because I typically had hiked longer days. Now that was about to change. If all went well, I would be able to resume hiking with Pilgrim and Dead Man in two days.

The 2,200-foot climb to Peak A of Wildcat Mountain (4,422 ft.) was tough. I had heard a few horror stories at the hostel about the mountain. I learned that just a few days ago a hiker fell trying to scale Wildcat Mountain and broke his hip. Much of my hike that day required rock scrambling. My foot searched for a toe hold while my fingers searched for a place on the rocks where I could get a grip. Often I had to pull my body up and over the rocks to higher ground. At one precarious time, I heard in my head my loving deceased mother call out to me saying, "Bobby, get down from there!" I politely answered, "Mom, I'll be glad to as soon as I can."

From Wildcat Mountain, there was over a 1,000-foot descent to the Carter Notch Hut (3,350 ft.). It was extremely wet around the hut and nearly impossible to avoid the deep puddles. The small hut is the most northern one on the trail. It was the fourth and final time that I enjoyed lunch at a hut. As usual, tasty soup was the order of the day. Only a section hiker and two staff were at the hut. By the time I had eaten, I sensed that the other hiker was a bit strange.

As I started to get ready to leave, so did the other hiker. I decided not to leave for several minutes, hoping he would go ahead of me. To my dismay, he delayed as well. Finally, I got up and walked to the door, and the other hiker closely followed behind me. After I had walked just a short distance from the hut, I asked him to pass me. He replied, "I would like to hike with you." That's wasn't what I wanted to hear. I said, "Well, I prefer to hike alone as I have been doing." He did not reply. I continued hiking for a few minutes, and he was just several steps behind me. Then I stopped, took a step off the trail, and asked him to pass me. After he did, I waited several minutes before resuming my hike. I became concerned a few minutes later when he was standing just a few steps off the trail. He appeared to be merely waiting for me.

I said, "I want you to know that it's not you. I just like to hike by myself." My comment was only partially true. I did like to hike by myself, but he made me feel ill at ease. I was hoping he would be appeased by my eloquence. However, he didn't say a word and gave me a cold stare. With that exchange, I felt the hair on my neck rise, and I felt very anxious. This was the only time on the trail when I became very wary of another hiker. Was this guy someone who could cause me harm? As I walked by him, I soon tried to pick up my pace. Occasionally, I would look back to see if he was in sight. Thankfully, he was not. I wondered if he were as uncomfortable with my reaction to him, as I was with him. To be on the safe side, I didn't take any breaks from hiking for a few hours.

In the late afternoon, I scaled Carter Dome (4,832 ft.). A short while later, I reached a small campsite at Mt. Hight (4,675 ft.), where Pilgrim told me that he and Dead Man had camped. Pilgrim recommended that I stay there. I could see the trail from the campsite, which was about 90 feet away. Just before I got into my tent, I saw the strange hiker approaching. I remained still and was partially obscured by trees. I stared at him as he walked by. However, he never looked in my direction. I didn't know if he had seen me, but I suspected he had. My feeling of concern arose again. Would he circle back after passing me? What was he thinking? Finally, I got over my paranoia and eventually went to sleep. Although I had hiked only about eight miles and had over 13 miles to hike to reach the hostel, the most difficult part of the 21-mile, two-day hike was over.

Day 140—Monday, August 8, 2011

As I awoke in the morning, my thoughts quickly went back to the day before and the hiker I tried to avoid. Although he didn't cause me any physical problem, he had been a major concern. I was thankful that I never saw him again. I was eager to reach the hostel, so I was hiking by 6:00. In the early morning, I descended to Zeta Pass (3,890 ft.) before climbing South Carter Mountain (4,458 ft.), Middle Carter Mountain (4,610 ft.), and North Carter Mountain (4,539 ft.). From there the trail descended about 1,300 feet before ascending 800 feet to Mt. Moriah (4,049 ft.). Rain had started by mid-morning and continued intermittently for several hours.

Around 3:30 the trail reached a stream. I could not find the white blaze for a few minutes as I wandered around looking for it. Finally, I felt relief as I spotted a white blaze and began following it. About 10 minutes later, I saw four hikers approaching me. Then I recognized one of the hikers. It was Portrait! I asked him why he was headed south on the trail. He looked at me askance and said, "We're heading north." I thought he was joking, but the other hikers supported his claim. I soon concluded that I was the one heading south—in the opposite direction that I should have been going.

As I turned around and headed north with the group, I was very embarrassed. In about 10 minutes, I was back at the stream where I had gotten turned around. I continued on with the group before they stopped at the Rattle River Shelter/Campsite (1,260 ft.). I thanked Portrait, as well as the entire group, for coming along and setting me straight. If they hadn't, I would have hiked much farther before discovering my mistake.

From the shelter/campsite, the trail descended about 500 feet in the next two miles. About 4:30, I reached U.S. 2 and turned left. After just a short walk on the road, I reached the White Mountains Lodge and Hostel. Pilgrim saw me coming down the road and was out to greet me. He was a welcome sight! I had a joyful feeling as I realized I had finally caught up with him and Dead Man. After dealing with rain earlier, it seemed appropriate that the sun was shining brightly. I put my tent and my boots outside to dry in the sun. After I took a shower, I was shuttled to a supermarket to resupply. Upon returning, Pilgrim, Dead Man and I were shuttled to a restaurant for dinner.

Day 141—Tuesday, August 9, 2011—Week 21

We enjoyed a good breakfast at the hostel, which was included in the price of our stay. About 6:20 we left, crossed U.S. 2, and began hiking. Within a few minutes, I noticed that Pilgrim and Dead Man were hiking at a slightly faster pace than I was. My ankle didn't hurt, but the new pace made me feel slightly uncomfortable and under pressure to keep up. Pilgrim took the lead position as he did when we hiked together. Dead Man asked me if I wanted to hike in the second position, but I chose to hike at the rear of the pack. I liked that position because I wouldn't slow Dead Man down, and I could see the line or path that he took hiking the trail.

Before I injured my ankle, I had to work hard on ascents to keep up with Pilgrim. However, at that time, I was actually faster than he was on descents. That had changed as I was now slower on both ascents and descents. Descents though were much harder on my ankle than climbing. Prior to my injury, Dead Man had been a slower hiker than Pilgrim and me and often hiked a shorter distance each day than we did. Now his pace was slightly faster than mine. When I fell behind Dead Man for more than 30 feet, I tried to hike faster and reduce the difference to about 15 feet. Pilgrim was much faster than both of us and often got so far ahead that he was out of sight. He would then wait at a location of his choosing for us to catch up.

I was very happy that Dead Man was part of our group. He was a delight to hike with. His self-deprecating humor made me laugh nearly every day. One example was when he said in an apologetic voice, "Feet, I know I have been beating you up every day for many months. I'm sorry! When I get home, I'll make it up to you. I promise." I wish I had written down many things that he said that made me laugh. I realized that if I had not injured my ankle, Dead Man would likely not have been hiking with us, so something good resulted from my ankle injury.

We climbed 1,800 feet up Mt. Hayes (2,555 ft.). In a few more miles, we reached Cascade Mountain (2,631 ft.) The climbs were not as tough as the earlier ones in the White Mountains, but they weren't easy. We descended over 500 feet to the Trident Col Tent Site (2,020 ft.) for lunch. In the afternoon, we passed two bodies of water with memorable names—Dream Lake (2,600 ft.) and Moss Pond (2,630 ft.). After hiking nearly 12 miles, we reached the Gentian Pond Shelter/Campsite (2,166 ft.), the last one in New Hampshire. With rain expected overnight, we all stayed in the large shelter, which slept 14. I reflected on the first day of resuming hiking with Pilgrim and Dead Man. It was a pleasant experience to have people I knew to hike with again. Given a little more time, I thought that likely I could readjust to their slightly faster pace.

Day 142—Wednesday, August 10, 2011

We started hiking at 6:40. It rained for most of the day, which made hiking much more difficult. We were either climbing or descending over slippery rocks, mud, and roots all day. Each of us fell numerous times, but no one was hurt. After we climbed Mt. Success (3,565 ft.), we began our descent to the New Hampshire/Maine border (2,972 ft.).

MAINE

I had completed 13 states on my AT hike (GA, NC, TN, VA, WV, MD, PA, NJ, NY, CT, MA, VT, and NH). Thirteen states down, one state to go! I still had to hike over 281 miles in Maine to reach the summit of Mt. Katahdin. Maine ranks second in the number of miles on the trail. Virginia is first with 550 miles.

Pilgrim, Dead Man and I had lunch at the Carlo Col Shelter (2,945 ft.). Then we went over Goose Eye Mountain (3,675 ft.) and experienced numerous rock scrambles. We had heard from other hikers that the terrain in southern Maine was perhaps tougher than in New Hampshire. After we had hiked nearly 10 miles, we reached the Full Goose Shelter/Campsite about 7:00. We hiked over 12 hours on the tiring day. We all agreed that hiking in Maine was difficult. After an all-day of rain, we decided to stay in the shelter.

Day 143—Thursday, August 11, 2011

It continued to rain overnight, but it had stopped by the morning. Pilgrim was apprehensive about hiking in bad weather in Mahoosuc Notch, which was only about a mile ahead. He thought that we should take a zero day and wait for better weather. Since Dead Man and I disagreed with him, Pilgrim reluctantly agreed to hike. We didn't begin hiking until 8:00 in order to make sure that the weather was favorable. We had a 400-foot climb and then immediately descended 1,000 feet and entered Mahoosuc Notch. It has a reputation as the toughest one mile on the entire AT. We climbed over, crawled under, squeezed between, slid down, and jumped from huge boulders. Nothing was easy. Many times the terrain looked impossible at first glance.

Many of the ascents and descents could have easily resulted in serious injury from a fall. At times we had to get on our hands and knees and pass our backpacks between each other just to get through the rock obstacles. By late morning, the sun was shining brightly. Surprisingly, we saw ice in deep crevices, which were shielded from the sun. We ate lunch sitting on a large, flat rock. It took us over three hours just to hike slightly more than one mile.

Pilgrim and Dead Man on the "trail" in Mahoosuc Notch, ME

After getting through Mahoosuc Notch, we climbed and scrambled for 1,600 feet to get over some sheer rock faces in an area called Mahoosuc Arm. We got to Speck Pond Shelter/Campsite (3,500 ft.) at 5:30. We set up our tents on a large platform. After nine hours on the trail, we had completed only five miles, the lowest mileage ever for a full day of hiking. We were satisfied though with the limited mileage because we did it without any injury. At the shelter/campsite, we talked with a young female section hiker who had suffered a deep gash on her leg in Mahoosuc Notch. She received medical treatment from the caretaker.

Day 144—Friday, August 12, 2011

We started hiking at 6:40 on a cool day. Soon we were making a steep 500-foot ascent requiring several rock scrambles. Then we needed to stop and put on our rain jackets as the weather changed abruptly. We were facing a misty rain and a wind that was swirling at about 30 mph. It quickly chilled the body and reduced visibility. After we reached the top of the climb, we began a descent of 2,500 feet. The weather was much improved at lower elevations. Next we climbed back up 2,300 feet to scale the West Peak of Baldpate Mountain (3,662 ft.). Once again the nasty weather temporarily returned.

After hiking nearly seven miles, we had lunch at the Baldpate Lean-to. In Maine, a lean-to is the popular term used to mean a shelter. Late in the day, we descended 1,500 feet to the Frye Notch Lean-to (2,280 ft.), where we set up our tents for the night. We had hiked over 10 miles. In the evening, we called the Pine Ellis Hostel in Andover to make a reservation for the following night. We were told to call for a shuttle when we reached East B Hill Road the next day.

Day 145—Saturday, August 13, 2011

The cool weather continued as we began hiking at 7:00. When we reached our pick-up point at 10:30, we called for a shuttle. After we arrived at the Pine Ellis Hostel, we did our laundry and had lunch at the Andover General Store. Pilgrim used a hot compress to treat a cut on his leg he had suffered in a fall. In the late afternoon, we were shuttled to a supermarket about ten miles from Andover to resupply. Pilgrim went to the store's pharmacy and sought an ointment for his leg wound. The pharmacist looked at the infected area and did not recommend any ointment. Instead, he told Pilgrim that he should see a doctor.

After we got into the vehicle to return to the hostel, Pilgrim told everyone what the pharmacist had said. The shuttle driver said that she could drive Pilgrim to see a doctor on Monday. It was nearly 6:00 on Saturday evening, and Monday was a long way off. I spoke up saying that the leg infection could be extremely severe by Monday, and Pilgrim needed medical attention now. I asked if there was a medical facility nearby. The driver said there was a hospital less than a mile away. A few minutes later, Pilgrim was in the emergency room. A doctor determined that he would need an antibiotic IV treatment. He was expected to be at the hospital for at least four hours.

Dead Man and I were then driven back to the hostel, but Pilgrim didn't return until 11:00. He announced that he would need to go back on Sunday morning to get the infection drained and have another antibiotic IV treatment. At that point, we knew that we would be taking a zero day on Sunday.

Day 146—Sunday, August 14, 2011

On Sunday morning it was raining as we all walked to the Andover General Store for breakfast. I was surprised and delighted to see Portrait there. He had hitched a ride to the store for breakfast. It was the last time I saw Portrait on the trail. After breakfast, Pilgrim was shuttled back to the hospital. When he returned in the late afternoon, he had a large gauze bandage covering the infection. The wound had been lanced and drained, and he had been given a second antibiotic IV treatment. Also, he received a ten-day supply of antibiotic pills, but he was cleared to resume hiking.

The rest of the day was spent at the hostel, enjoying the leisure time and reviewing information about the remainder of the hike. I spoke to Cindi about a story on the internet that a thru-hiker's body was found near the 2,000-mile mark on the trail. The hiker's name was Iron Mike, and his death appeared to be due to natural causes as no foul play was suspected. We were about 65 miles south of the location where the body was found.

Day 147—Monday, August 15, 2011

I was eating breakfast at the kitchen table of the hostel early in the morning when Dead Man appeared. He said, "I have bad news. Pilgrim just told me that his leg really hurts, and he is going home." I was shocked. Then Dead Man proposed a plan, which he thought Pilgrim might approve. It involved Pilgrim taking some over-the-counter pain medication, such as Advil. When his pain had subsided, the three of us could slackpack for about 10 miles. Then we could be picked up and shuttled back to the hostel. The next day, Pilgrim could decide if he was able and willing to continue hiking, or he could decide to go home. Pilgrim heard Dead Man's plan and agreed to give it a try.

At 7:00 we were shuttled back to East B Hill Road. We carried water and our lunch in a small backpack, which we borrowed from the hostel. We wore rain pants and rain jackets on a dismal rainy day. The trail was muddy, rocky, and slippery as ice, and we all fell at least once. We began with a 1,500-foot ascent up Wyman Mountain (2,920 ft.). We stopped for lunch at the Hall Mountain Shelter (2,634 ft.). Then about 2:00, as we were instructed, we stopped, called the hostel, and gave our location. Next we descended 1,800 feet before climbing to the top of Moody Mountain (2,460 ft.). Our final descent brought us to S. Arm Road about 3:30. The van, waiting to shuttle us back to the Pine Ellis Hostel, was a welcome sight. The pain medication that Pilgrim took had worked well. The day was a real success.

At the hostel, we did a communal load of laundry, consisting of the wet and muddy clothes that we had just worn. Every hostel has some clothes for hikers to wear while they do laundry. I put on a pair of blue jean shorts, which were made for a man with a waist twice my size. I had to hold up the shorts as I walked, or they would have been at my ankles. I was glad to get my own clean, dry clothes back.

There were a few familiar faces at the hostel. One hiker, whom I had met previously, was Chainsaw. He was a retired firefighter from Baltimore County, Maryland. He got his trail name because when he snored, it apparently sounded like someone was operating a chainsaw! For supper we went back to the Andover General Store. Some of the men hanging around the store began to recognize our familiar faces. We were becoming honorary citizens of Andover.

Day 148—Tuesday, August 16, 2011—Week 22

After a three-night stay, we said goodbye to the Pine Ellis Hostel and Andover as we were shuttled back to S. Arm Road at 8:00. A light rain fell as we began hiking. Since it had rained for several days, the trail at times resembled a creek. After an hour or so of hiking, it was futile to try to avoid stepping in water. My boots were already pretty well soaked. The trail was downright ugly. It was nearly impossible not to step on a tree root every few feet. I called tree roots the number one enemy of thru-hikers because it was so easy to trip over even a small one.

The shuttle driver told us that Old Blue Mountain (3,600 ft.) was steep and tough. He was correct, although my impression was that Moody Mountain, which we had climbed the day before, was just as challenging. There was plenty of rock scrambling, and we used the bars that were imbedded into the rock as well as ladders to scale the heights. They made it easier to get up and over the boulders. Later in the afternoon, after a long and difficult descent, we climbed Bemis Mountain (3,580 ft.). After hiking less than nine miles for the day, we reached the Bemis Lean-to (2,790 ft.) about 5:00. Since it wasn't raining, I set up my tent. Pilgrim and Dead Man elected to stay in the shelter.

Day 149—Wednesday, August 17, 2011

It rained overnight, but it stopped by morning. We began hiking at 7:00 on a nice day. Soon we faced a tough and steep descent of 1,300 feet, followed by a 1,000-foot ascent with rock scrambles, ladders, and metal bars. We had lunch sitting on a rock at a high elevation with a lovely view of a large pond well below. Hiking in the afternoon was relatively easy.

When we reached Little Swift River Pond at 5:30, we had hiked nearly 13 miles. All of us set up our tents and enjoyed what was left of the sunny day. Maine is truly a gorgeous state, and it is easy to be impressed by its beautiful wilderness. At higher elevations, there are great vistas of ponds and a blanket of green.

Day 150—Thursday, August 18, 2011

It was a beautiful day with the sun shining as we began hiking at 7:00. We experienced descents of 800 and 900 feet before climbing 2,600 feet to go over Saddleback Mountain (4,120 ft.) in the afternoon. Then we descended nearly 1,000 feet before climbing The Horn (3,904 ft.). Both mountains offered spectacular views of Maine in all directions. Finally, we descended 900 feet to the Redington Stream Campsite, where all of us were eager to set up our tents for the night. We were the only hikers there. We had hiked slightly more than 13 miles. It is easy to recommend Maine as an excellent place for R and R—not only for rest and relaxation but for roots and rocks.

Day 151—Friday, August 19, 2011

We were blessed again with yet another lovely day, the third day in a row. We began hiking at 7:00. Soon we were climbing Saddleback Junior Mountain (3,655 ft.), an elevation 465 feet less than its higher senior relative. We forded three streams before lunch. The depth of the water ranged from just above the ankle to slightly above the waist. Preparing to ford a stream involved a five-minute procedure of removing socks and boots, putting on crocs, and unloosening back-packs. Upon fording a stream, another five-minute ordeal was necessary before hiking could resume.

The mud on the trail was still a minor problem, but far better than earlier in the week. In mid-afternoon, we stopped at the Spaulding Mountain Lean-to (3,140 ft.), where we decided to take a break to eat and rest. As we were finishing a snack, a retired couple reached the lean-to. They spoke of enjoying their conversation the previous week with Iron Mike, just one day before he had died on the trail. They also spoke of the many peaks of Bigelow Mountain, a very difficult part of the trail we would soon face.

About 4:00 we resumed hiking, aiming for a small campsite at the South Branch of the Carrabassett River just over five miles ahead. To get there, we climbed Spaulding Mountain (4,000 ft.) and then descended 1,900 feet to the campsite. We arrived at 7:45, and it was dark by the time we had set up our tents. Once again we were the only hikers at the campsite. It was a good day of hiking, and we were pleased with having hiked over 15 miles in the nearly 13-hour day. Mt. Katahdin was less than 200 miles away.

Day 152—Saturday, August 20, 2011

We started our hike at 7:00 on another beautiful day. In the first few miles, we climbed about 2,000 feet to reach South Crocker Mountain (4,039 ft.). After descending 400 feet, we scaled North Crocker Mountain (4,228 ft.). Over the next five miles, we descended 2,800-feet to reach ME 27 at 2:30. Although we had hiked nearly nine miles, we were still five miles from our destination of the Stratton Motel & Hostel in Stratton, Maine (population 488).

Dead Man attempted to hitch a ride for us into Stratton, but the traffic was light. We were not about to walk five miles along the narrow winding road in the mid-day sun. After an hour, we finally got a ride into Stratton. During the drive, we held our backpacks on our laps.

After getting our room, we put our damp gear outside to dry. As usual, Dead Man took our dirty clothes to the laundry. Then we went to the White Wolf Café to eat lunch. In the evening, we went back to the same restaurant for a delicious dinner. I paid the bill in appreciation of Pilgrim and Dead Man taking a zero day so that I could catch up with them in New Hampshire.

Day 153—Sunday, August 21, 2011

We took a zero day, which we thought would probably be our last one on the hike. We started the day by enjoying a great breakfast at the Stratton Diner, directly across the street. Then we resupplied at Fotter's Market. We bought enough food for eight days to get us from Stratton to Monson, Maine, our next available resupply point. Since we did not want to carry that much food, we shipped half of it to a lodge near Caratunk, where we planned to stay in four days.

My Scarpa boots had little tread and had split at the sole. I had worn them for 1,973 miles on the AT, but I had hoped to wear them the entire hike. Although they had given me great service, they needed badly to be replaced.

My Scarpa boots had taken a beating on the AT!

After lunch, the owner of the hostel drove me to an outfitter in Rangely, where I bought new comfortable Merrill boots.

Day 154—Monday, August 22, 2011

We ate breakfast in our room before we were shuttled to the trailhead at 7:00. We did a lot of climbing in the Bigelow Mountain Range. From Stratton

Brook (1,230 ft.), we ascended 2,600 feet to South Horn (3,831 ft.). Then we scaled the West Peak (4,145 ft.) before reaching the Avery Peak (4,090 ft.). The weather was nice for much of the day until we were climbing the West Peak. We put on rain jackets then as it became cold and windy with a light mist. From Avery Peak, we descended over 1,800 feet to the Safford Notch Campsite (2,230 ft.). We camped there at 5:00, after hiking over 10 miles. I was pleased that I had completed over 2,000 miles on the AT.

Day 155—Tuesday, August 23, 2011—Week 23

It was a cool morning as we started hiking at 7:00. We ascended about 800 feet to the east end of Little Bigelow Mountain (3,010 ft.). Then we began a descent of 1,250 feet to the Little Bigelow Lean-to (1,760 ft.), where we had lunch. Next we descended 600 feet to the foot of the serene Flagstaff Lake, where we had a lengthy rest in the shade.

We resumed hiking and came to the Long Falls Dam Road, where 2,000 miles was written in white paint. However, we had actually completed hiking 2,000 miles late the day before. Since the length of the AT changes slightly each year, the mile marker was now incorrect. I thought of Iron Mike, who had died about two weeks earlier, very close to where we were.

We had one more climb of over 500 feet up Roundtop Mountain (1,760 ft.) before the final descent of over 400 feet. At 5:00 we reached the West Carry Pond Lean-to (1,340 ft.), where we set up camp. We had hiked over 12 miles. We got a true feeling of nature after dinner as we heard the eerie yodel of the common loons on the large pond.

Day 156—Wednesday, August 24, 2011

We began hiking at 7:00 on a nice day. It was probably the easiest day of hiking that we had in Maine. The elevation changes on the trail were moderate, varying by no more than 200 feet at a time, but there were still plenty of rocks, roots, and mud. In the morning, we met two women (Shuffle and Dash) who were section hikers. They raved about having eaten a fantastic breakfast at Harrison Pierce Pond Camp.

We reached the Pierce Pond Lean-to (1,150 ft.) in mid-afternoon and set up our tents. It was a welcome change to simply relax and enjoy the remainder of the day. Pierce Pond, like many others, was quite large. The ponds in Maine are often hundreds of acres, and they look more like a good-sized lake. They are in the wilderness, surrounded by trees, and absolutely gorgeous. Late in the day we made a breakfast reservation for the next morning at the Harrison Pierce Pond Camp.

Day 157—Thursday, August 25, 2011

We left camp at 6:30 and hiked about a half mile to the rustic Harrison Pierce Pond Camp built in 1934. It was decorated with a sportsman's flair for fishermen and vacationers. The highlight of the fantastic breakfast was the delicious pancakes—the best I have ever eaten. They were loaded with juicy blueberries and tiny pieces of apple, topped with confectionary sugar. Within five minutes of leaving the camp, we saw a moose about 60 feet away, standing in a small pond just below the trail. Wow, what a huge animal!

A moose enjoying breakfast in Maine

Soon we reached the Kennebec River, the most formidable water-crossing on the AT. The river spans 150 yards and is up to six feet deep. A thru-hiker drowned in 1985 trying to ford the dangerous river, and many others have had close calls. To get across the water, hikers are strongly urged to use the free ferry service. The ferry is actually a canoe, which has a white blaze painted on the bottom to mark the official AT route. From mid-July to late September, hikers and their packs are transported between the hours of 9-11 a.m. and 2-4 p.m. We reached the river before 10:00. We became part of the tens of thousands of hikers over the last several decades to use the ferry service.

Ferry service for hikers across the Kennebec River in Maine

After we crossed the river, we hiked a short distance to reach U.S. 201 in Caratunk (population 75). That marked the end of our short and easy day of hiking as we completed four miles. For over an hour, we tried unsuccessfully to hitch a ride to the Northern Outdoors Resort a few miles down the road. Eventually, we were picked up by the same man who had ferried us across the Kennebec River. He drove us to the lodge, where we had a reservation for the night. Each of us picked up the four-day supply of food that we had shipped from Stratton earlier in the week. The resort offers class IV rafting trips on the Kennebec River. At the bustling lodge, we shared a room and enjoyed lunch and dinner. In the evening, we arranged for a ride back to the trail in the early morning.

Day 158—Friday, August 26, 2011

After we had breakfast in our room, a staff member drove us back to the trail at 6:15. It was a nice day, and we began to wonder if the good weather would last the rest of the hike. We had a long climb of 1,900 feet to the top of Pleasant Pond Mountain (2,470 ft.), where we had an early lunch and enjoyed an impressive view on the clear day. After lunch, we descended 1,500 feet to Moxie Pond (970 ft.). Then we forded Baker Stream, where the water was knee-high with a strong current. Finally, we had an ascent of more than 300 feet to reach Bald Mountain Brook Lean-to (1,280 ft.), where we set up our tents about 4:30. We had hiked nearly 15 miles.

Day 159—Saturday, August 27, 2011

It was hard to believe, but the weather was wonderful yet again. We began hiking at 6:30. In the first two miles of the hike, we climbed 1,350 feet to the top of Moxie Bald Mountain (2,629 ft.). From there, we looked down on the low-lying clouds over Moxie Pond. Then over the next eight miles, we descended over 1,700 feet. During the day, we forded two more bodies of water. At the Bald Mountain Pond, the water level was at mid-calf, while at the West Branch of the Piscataquis River, it was knee deep. Although the mud had diminished due to the streak of good weather, there were the usual rocks and tree roots. After hiking 13 miles, we reached the Horseshoe Canyon Lean-to (880 ft.) about 3:30.

I set up my tent behind the shelter, while Pilgrim and Dead Man decided to stay in the lean-to. About 5:00, I called Cindi and asked her to check the weather forecast for me. She said that rain was 100% certain for the area from about midnight through the following day. The primary cause of rain and severe weather was Hurricane Irene. Because of that information, I took down my tent and moved into the lean-to. About 8:00 the rain started, and the wind picked up. Sometime after dark, we heard a loud bang when a large tree branch fell on the metal roof of the shelter.

Day 160—Sunday, August 28, 2011

In the morning, we could see a big dent in the roof from the fallen branch. Our destination was Shaw's Lodging in Monson (population 686), which was nine miles ahead. We were eager to get an early start, so we began hiking at 6:15. The rain was moderate but steady all morning. However, we knew that Hurricane Irene would bring much more rain and flooding.

We were anxious to ford the East Branch of the Piscataquis River, which was a little more than two miles ahead. The guide book said it was a dangerous river to ford after much rain. A benefit of the dry weather we had experienced for much of the past two weeks was that the water level of the rivers and streams had dropped prior to the current rain. When we reached the Piscataquis River, we were relieved that the water level was only at mid-calf. The overnight rain, though, had made the trail muddier and more slippery.

When we were a few miles from ME 15, we called Shaw's Lodging to request a shuttle to pick us up there about 11:30. When we were just 100 yards from ME 15, Dead Man's feet went out from underneath him on a descent. He was hiking over a flat, sloping rock, and he landed on his tail bone. He let out a painful cry. He sat for a minute before getting up and slowly walking to the road. His fall brought back memories of my similar accident on North Kinsman Mountain, which was exactly one month earlier.

After hiking nine miles, it was a pleasure to board the shuttle, escape the rain, and head to the well-respected hostel. Once there, I got my own room, while Pilgrim and Dead Man shared a double room across the hall. I met several hikers whom I hadn't seen for a while, including Old Granddad and Chainsaw. It felt great to renew old acquaintances. Rain continued to fall in the evening and overnight.

Day 161—Monday, August 29, 2011

In the morning, we heard that the East Branch of the Piscataquis River, which we had forded at the mid-calf level just the day before, was now impassible. Wow! If we had not forded the river when we did, we would have had to wait days for the water to recede.

We were in the area known as the "100-Mile Wilderness," which starts near Monson and ends at Abol Bridge, just south of Baxter State Park. It is the longest stretch of wilderness on the AT. Although several logging roads cross the AT in the wilderness, a hiker can go nearly 100 miles without seeing a car. The rugged and remote area has pristine ponds and lakes and offers beautiful vistas.

Shaw's Lodging has a great reputation for its breakfasts. A hiker may order up to five of each item (eggs, bacon, sausage, and pancakes) served. The only stipulation is that a hiker must eat whatever he orders. I ordered four of each item as I was sure I could eat that much. After the hearty breakfast, I was ready to hike.

At 8:30 Pilgrim, Dead Man, Chainsaw, and I were shuttled several miles to our starting point. Old Granddad had done the same hike the day before, so he took a zero day. In order to avoid dangerous streams farther north, we flip flopped and hiked six miles back toward Shaw's Lodging. We carried only food and water needed for the day. We had lunch at the Leeman Brook Lean-to (1,070 ft.). The trail in many spots resembled a small creek. When we reached Leeman Brook, it had risen greatly. It usually contains only a trickle of water, but when we got there, the water level was mid-calf and rushing. We forded it cautiously. In the early afternoon, we reached ME 15 and called for a shuttle to take us back to the hostel.

In the later afternoon, we were driven several miles to a supermarket to resupply. We bought enough food for eight days to get us through the 100-mile wilderness. At the end of the day, Old Granddad, Chainsaw, Pilgrim, Dead Man, and I agreed to hike together to Mt. Katahdin and formatted a new strategy to get us through the 100-mile wilderness.

Day 162 — Tuesday, August 30, 2011 — Week 24

Hurricane Irene had resulted in impassible bodies of water beginning six miles north of Monson. We wanted to avoid that high water until it had the chance to recede. Since there were fewer and smaller streams farther north in the wilderness, the five of us were shuttled 52 miles north and dropped off at Jo-Mary Road, a logging road that crosses the AT.

About 10:00 we began hiking south toward Monson carrying a four-day supply of food as we expected to arrive back at Shaw's in four days. After we had hiked a little more than six miles, we stopped at the Cooper Brook Falls Lean-to (910 ft.) and ate lunch. Then we had over a 1,000-foot ascent to Little Boardman Mountain (1,980 ft.) before we descended to the East Branch of the Pleasant River (1,200 ft.). Although the water level was waist deep with a strong current, we were able to ford the river very slowly with extreme caution. The water came up to the bottom of my backpack, and my gear got slightly wet. Finally, we had over a 1,300-foot ascent to the Logan Brook Lean-to (2,530 ft.). We arrived there at 7:15 and set up our tents. Even though we didn't start hiking until mid-morning, we had covered over 15 miles.

Day 163 — Wednesday, August 31, 2011

We began hiking at 6:45 on a cool, dry day. After hiking about a mile, we entered an area called the White Cap Range. Our first ascent of over 1,100 feet took us to the top of White Cap Mountain (3,650 ft.). Next we descended over 500 feet before we climbed Hay Mountain (3,244 ft.). Then we descended over 800 feet before reaching Gulf Hagas (2,683 ft.), a gorge that is often called the Grand Canyon of the East.

At that point, we began a descent of over 2,000 feet to the West Branch of the Pleasant River (680 ft.). We forded the waist-deep water. Finally, we began our last climb of the day of 1,000 feet to reach East Chairback Pond (1,630 ft.) at 6:00. Good campsites were at a premium there as we searched for a level place to set up our tents. I spent more than 10 minutes before finding an adequate site. We had hiked nearly 15 miles.

Day 164 — Thursday, September 1, 2011

Since Hurricane Irene had passed by, the weather was quite nice on the trail. We began hiking at 6:45 on a great day that I called "mountain-climbing day" since we climbed five mountains in the Barren-Chairback Range. None of the mountains was particularly high in elevation. However, each time we climbed one, we had a lengthy, rugged descent before climbing the next. The mountains we climbed were: Chairback Mountain (2,180 ft.), Columbus Mountain (2,325 ft.), Third Mountain (1,920 ft.), Fourth Mountain (2,380 ft.), and Barren Mountain (2,660 ft.).

I laughed at two of the mountains having just a number—third and fourth. When the mountains were first identified, there may have been more mountains than people in Maine. Whoever named the mountains may have said, "Let's just call two of the mountains by a number. If there are a few famous people from Maine in the future, Third Mountain and Fourth Mountain can be renamed after them."

During the day, we didn't have to ford any bodies of water. After hiking nearly 14 miles over 11 hours, we reached the Long Pond Stream Lean-to (930 ft.) at 6:15. Although we were all tired, we were relieved and pleased to have scaled five mountains during the long day. Since the weather remained pleasant, we set up our tents for the night.

Day 165—Friday, September 2, 2011

Our hike began at 6:30 on a beautiful day. There were no mountains to climb like the day before, but there were plenty of ascents and descents of hundreds of feet at a time. We forded three bodies of water: Long Pond Stream (thigh high), Big Wilson Stream (knee high), and Little Wilson Stream (calf high). It was refreshing to ford a stream with cold water, but it was time consuming. We were relieved that each of the streams was passable. There was a sense of satisfaction from just getting across each body of water safely.

Fording a stream in Maine

Earlier in the week, we would not have been able to ford those streams. Of course, that is why we were shuttled north to hike back south toward Monson. Our strategy to keep hiking and avoid the high water worked as planned.

We hiked about nine miles and arrived at 2:00 at the pick-up point. By mid-afternoon, we were back at Shaw's Lodging. We showered, did laundry, charged our batteries, packed our remaining four-day food supply, ate dinner, and got a good night's sleep.

Day 166—Saturday, September 3, 2011

As we sat down for breakfast at Shaw's Lodging, I decided to order five of every item served. I was able to eat everything on my plate. Then we were shuttled 52 miles back to Jo-Mary Road, one hour and forty-five minutes away. This time we headed north on the AT toward Mt. Katahdin, and we carried our remaining four-day food supply to get us through the wilderness. We had spent three nights in total at Shaw's Lodging. All of us were grateful to Dawn and Dick at Shaw's Lodging for their assistance in helping us plan and carry out our safe passage through the 100-Mile Wilderness.

The elevation changes for the day were very moderate. It was a pretty easy day of hiking except for one mishap, which resulted from fording a stream. We forded the first stream in the typical manner by removing our socks and boots and putting on crocs. However, at the second stream, there were a number of decent-sized rocks in the water. Pilgrim suggested that it was possible to get across without removing our boots. He went first. Although I did not feel really comfortable attempting to rock hop across, I started to cross when Pilgrim was about half way to the other side. Unfortunately, about 2/3 of the way across, I fell into the swift stream. In a moment, my right foot was trapped between two rocks, and water was gushing at me. I was waist deep in the water, and the strong current made it difficult to stand upright. I dropped my hiking sticks as I tried to regain my balance and get my foot out from between the rocks. It took me about 20 seconds to regain complete control of the precarious situation.

At that point, I trudged to the shore on the far side of the stream and took off my backpack. My one hiking stick was accessible, and I went back into the stream to get it. However, the other hiking stick had disappeared below the cold water. Dead Man was on the opposite shore and had not yet begun to cross. He was at a higher elevation and could see one of my hiking sticks about 50 feet downstream on the bottom. He guided me verbally to the point where eventually I could see it below the water. I reached down and pulled it out.

After the rather scary episode had ended, Dead Man smartly removed his socks and shoes and proceeded to ford the stream in a safer manner. The bottom of my backpack had been in the water. Later when I checked on the items in my pack, they were mostly dry. No real harm was done, and I continued to wear the drenched clothes and wet boots the rest of the day. The lesson I learned was to proceed cautiously in fording a stream. We continued hiking until 6:30 when we camped just off the trail. Considering the late morning start, we were pleased to have hiked 15 miles.

Day 167—Sunday, September 4, 2011

We started hiking at 6:30 and soon climbed 900 feet to the top of Nesunt-abunt Mountain (1,520 ft.) before descending about 900 feet to Pollywog Stream (682 ft.). The morning was difficult with lots of mud and unending standing water. We forded one small stream by rock hopping. We did not take off our boots to put on crocs because if anyone of us had fallen in the shallow water, the worst thing that could have happened was wet feet.

About noon we stopped for lunch at the Rainbow Stream Lean-to (1,005 ft.). The afternoon had easier terrain with no major climbs, but mud and water were everywhere. At 3:30 we heard thunder in the distance, and it kept creeping closer. At 4:30 we reached Rainbow Spring Campground (1,100 ft.), just as the rain began. We hiked nearly 15 miles.

Unfortunately, everyone had to set up their tents in the steady rain. I moved as fast as possible, but the inside of my tent got fairly wet. I used my chamois cloth to try to mop up a few small puddles. As the rain continued, I ate dinner in my tent. The rain stopped in the early evening, and I quickly walked to a nearby spring close to the shore of Rainbow Lake to get water.

Day 168—Monday, September 5, 2011

Heavy rain overnight left us with wet tents and damp gear, and it was still raining lightly in the morning. Soon I heard some grumbling from two of my hiking companions about the rain. Although I was not thrilled with the weather, I said that we should not get down or be depressed because of rain. I stressed focusing on the positive, not the negative. In the big picture, we were closing in on our goal, and all was well! Pilgrim thanked me for my positive outlook.

We began hiking at 7:00. Our objective was to reach Abol Bridge, a distance of slightly more than 11 miles. The trail was very sloppy, and we had to hike through mud most of the day. We reached Abol Bridge at 2:30. We got a sandwich and drink at a small retail store. Since we wanted to spend the night indoors to regroup, we called the Appalachian Trail Lodge in Millinocket (population 4,456) to pick us up. The shuttle arrived about 3:00 and drove us to the hostel, which was about 20 miles away.

After arriving there, we showered, dried our shoes and gear, and bought food for the next few days. We walked to the Appalachian Trail Café for dinner. It rained hard in the evening, and it was expected to continue the following day. We reviewed our options for the next few days. We decided to hike to the Katahdin

Stream Campsite at the foot of Mt. Katahdin the next day. Then on Wednesday, we planned to climb Mt. Katahdin.

Day 169—Tuesday, September 6, 2011—Week 25

At 9:00 we were shuttled back to Abol Bridge. The weather was surprisingly dry the whole day. We had lunch sitting along the Nesowadnehunk Stream. It was raging and looked deep and furious. Fortunately, we didn't have to ford the stream because we would not have been able to do so. The raging water was at least chest high and would have washed away any hiker.

After hiking about 10 miles, we reached Katahdin Stream Campsite at the base of the mountain at 2:15. The summit of Mt. Katahdin was less than six miles away and within sight.

Mt. Katahdin from Katahdin Stream Campground in Maine

We went to the Ranger Station, which is located at the campground, and registered as thru-hikers. We each selected a small backpack there to use on our hike up Mt. Katahdin the next day. It is strongly suggested that each hiker leave his own backpack on the porch of the Ranger Station before attempting to climb the mountain.

We each paid $10 to camp. Pilgrim and Dead Man shared a small, two-person lean-to, while I shared a similar one with Old Granddad. Chainsaw tented nearby. We had plenty of time to collect our thoughts and prepare for the final day of our long hike. It seemed appropriate that the translation of the Indian word Katahdin is "greatest." We were just a day away from climbing Maine's highest and "greatest mountain!"

Day 170—Wednesday, September 7, 2011

We were up early and eager to begin our climb to the summit of Mt. Katahdin (5,268 ft.). We started up the mountain just before 6:00. The weather was cool, and later in the morning, it began to rain very lightly. As we proceeded up the mile-high mountain, Old Granddad and Chainsaw hiked at a faster pace. As the elevation increased, the wind gradually picked up, and the temperature continued to drop. As we were very near the summit, we met Old Granddad and Chainsaw on their descent. They had reached the summit well before us. After we exchanged greetings, they continued down the mountain. At the summit, Old Granddad shared with Chainsaw the small bottle of Old Grand-Dad Whiskey he had carried on the hike.

After a cold and difficult climb, Pilgrim, Dead Man and I reached the summit at 11:00. It was as if the old mountain was saying to us, "You didn't think it would be easy, did you?" My answer would have been, "Of course not!" We stayed at the summit for about 15 minutes. Dead Man emotionally read a brief scripture passage praising God for watching over us and guiding us safely on our journey. Then we all took a few photos and had a snack.

I'm sure that we would have stayed longer at the summit, if the weather had been milder. The wind chill made it feel like about 30 degrees.

Although we had reached our goal of climbing Mt. Katahdin, we still had over five miles of the dangerous mountain trail to descend. Because the descent is not considered part of the 2,181-mile thru-hike, Dead Man had joked that he wanted to rent a helicopter to transport us off the mountain. His silly idea made sense to me since my hands were numb as I started down. I tried rubbing them together, holding hiking sticks under my arm. I chastised myself for not having brought gloves, which I left in my backpack at the Ranger Station. We were concerned that a fall on the way down would certainly spoil the otherwise great day, so we proceeded cautiously.

After we had descended nearly a mile, we met Swift, Nachita, and Poncho. Although I had last seen Swift about six days before on the trail, I hadn't seen Nachita and Poncho since Vermont. The farther we hiked down the mountain, the more the weather continually improved. About halfway down, we reached an area where the rocks sheltered us from the wind. We stopped there and ate lunch.

SUCCESS on the journey of hope! 9/7/11

As we resumed hiking, we felt a real spring in our step, infused by the realization of a successful climb of Mt. Katahdin.

We reached the Ranger Station just before 4:00 and claimed our backpacks. Old Granddad and Chainsaw were waiting for us. The shuttle to the Appalachian Trail Lodge had also arrived. A few minutes later, we began our ride back to the hostel in Millinocket. After we showered, we went to a restaurant for dinner. After supper, we spent several minutes talking with Swift, Nachita, and Poncho.

The night was a joyous celebration of hard work, determination, and good fortune granted by the grace of God. Our entire group, which we jokingly called the Geriatric Hiking Club or GHC for short, was thankful for having hiked with each other. I returned from dinner and prepared my backpack for departure after breakfast. I tried to soak in the fact that I had hiked 2,181 miles from Georgia to Maine on the Appalachian Trail over 170 days! I had only one thought in my mind at bedtime. My dream had become a reality. God had blessed me with an adventure of a lifetime on this journey of hope!

AFTER THE HIKE

Day 171—Thursday, September 8, 2011

Pilgrim, Dead Man, Old Granddad, Chainsaw, and I went to breakfast at the Appalachian Trail Café in Millinocket. After we had ordered breakfast, we wrote our names on a ceiling tile for having completed hiking the entire length of the AT in 2011. I recognized the names of many hikers who had previously signed the ceiling tile.

Chainsaw had a friend who was picking him up after breakfast. The rest of us were shuttled to Medway, Maine, and dropped off at a gas station. We bought bus tickets there to our desired destinations. Dead Man and I boarded a Concord Motor Coach to nearby Bangor, while Pilgrim and Old Granddad headed southeast. Dead Man and I arrived at the bus terminal in Bangor about 11:00. We called for a shuttle to the Days Inn.

After we got our motel room, we were shuttled to the Bangor Airport, to rent a car. We drove about an hour to Acadia National Park along the rugged coast of Maine. It was the first national park east of the Mississippi River. We thoroughly enjoyed touring the park and seeing gorgeous views from the granite peaks. By late afternoon, we headed to Bar Harbor to walk its streets, visit some stores, and enjoy dinner. After a pleasant and worthwhile trip, we returned to Bangor at dark.

Day 172—Friday, September 9, 2011

Following a continental breakfast at the motel, we loaded our belongings into the rental car and drove to the airport. After we returned the rental car, I called Dr. Kim Brown. I told him what a tremendous help he was to me after I injured my ankle. He suggested that I still get my ankle x-rayed when I got home. Dead Man and I were on the same flight to Philadelphia. From there Dead Man flew to Atlanta, and I flew to Cleveland. After being away for such a long time, it felt good to arrive home.

Q & A

How much did the thru-hike cost you?

The cost of my thru-hike was approximately $8,500, including food ($4,200), equipment and clothes ($2,600), lodging ($700), air fares ($500), cell phone ($400), and miscellaneous expenses ($100).

What items did you carry in your backpack?

The long list included pack cover, tent, rain fly, tent stakes, ground cover, air mattress, sleeping bag, Camelbak, water bottle, cup, quart pan and lid, stove, fuel canister, lighter, utensils, food/snacks, crocs, cell phone, camera, chargers for phone/camera, socks, briefs, long underwear, pants, shorts, shirts, fleece jacket, rain jacket, rain pants, wide brim hat, baseball hat, knit hat, bandana, gloves, headlamp, small flashlight, extra batteries, dishwashing detergent, small sponge, hand sanitizer, pocket knife, reading glasses, sun glasses, moleskin, insect repellant, chamois cloth, pain medication, band aids, toilet paper, tooth brush, tooth paste, dental floss, nail clippers, and comb. Although I started the hike carrying a water filter, soon I replaced it with Aqua Mira.

Which part of the trail did you like best?

I enjoyed all parts of the trail, but the one state that especially impressed me was Maine. Its mountains and wilderness, coupled with its trees and numerous ponds, were beautiful and serene.

What did you miss the most on your hike?

I missed my grandchildren greatly because they were changing the most while I was gone. I missed being able to be clean most of the time. Although I often used hand sanitizers, I really would have liked to have washed my hands more often.

How was the cell phone service on the trail?

I used Verizon for cell phone service. It had the best reputation for being able to make a connection. I was able to get service about 70% of the time. To conserve power, I kept my phone off until I wanted to make a call. I was able to charge the phone whenever I was at a location that had electric power, such as a hostel, motel, or restaurant.

How many hikers completed a thru-hike in 2011?

The ATC reported that in 2011 there were 1,700 aspiring thru-hikers, of which 414 hikers or 24.4% were successful. The result was similar in 2010 when the ATC reported that there were 1,460 aspiring thru-hikers, of which 349 hikers or 23.9% were successful.

What are the biggest factors that you think determine whether a person would be able to complete a thru-hike of the AT?

Determination and good health are both major factors of a successful thru-hike. Determination keeps a physically and mentally tired hiker moving ahead when the trail is difficult. It certainly helps to be in good physical condition before starting. I believe that a person with a chronic knee problem would be unlikely to thru-hike the trail. Of course, a severe injury can end any hiker's dream. It is important to start slowly and gradually increase the distance one hikes.

If you could do it over, what would you do differently?

To save time and money, I would have gone to an outfitter that employed an experienced long-distance thru-hiker as a salesperson. Next I would have put all my "stuff" in my backpack, weighed it, and then taken a hike to see if I could carry it comfortably. Finally, I would carry an Aircast Air-Stirrup ankle brace, which is light and compact. Since foot injuries are very common on the hike, it makes sense to be ready to deal with a severe sprain or even a break.

Were there many women attempting to thru-hike the AT?

About 20% of aspiring thru-hikers were women. I was impressed by most of the female hikers I met. They were strong and displayed real determination.

Did you find any parts of the hike boring?

Although I didn't find any part of the hike boring, some parts of the trail were less interesting than others. However, there usually was something different about each part.

Did you ever seriously consider quitting the hike?

I never considered quitting. However, there were a few times when I wished that I had not seen the video on television about thru-hiking the AT. Those trying times occurred after I injured my ankle when the trail was most difficult.

SOME FINAL THOUGHTS

Ten days after I arrived back in Cleveland, my ankle was still slightly swollen and tender. It had been nearly two months since I had injured it on July 28 when I fell on a descent on North Kinsman Mountain in the White Mountains of New Hampshire. I made an appointment to see an orthopedic specialist, Dr. Robert Coale. At his office, an x-ray technician took three x-rays. Within a few minutes, the technician came into the examination room where I was waiting to see the doctor. With an expression of wonderment she said, "Do you know you have a broken ankle?" "No, I did not, but I am not really surprised," I replied.

When the doctor entered the office, I told him my AT tale. He was quite surprised that I was able to continue hiking after just a few days of rest, especially in the rugged terrain of the White Mountains. He said that I must have a high level of pain tolerance, but I never thought that I did. He described the break as an "oblique distal fibula fracture." He advised me not to run or jog for another four weeks. He described the break as clean and mostly healed. He said that in four-to-six more weeks the ankle should be fully healed and pretty much back to normal. As I reflected on the injury, I was glad that I didn't know that it was broken. If I had, I most likely would have taken several weeks off and gone home. I believe the old saying is true, "All's well that ends well!"

When I spoke with Dead Man some time later, I learned that he had actually broken his tailbone on his fall in Maine. The AT was responsible for the broken bones that Dead Man and I suffered and for Pilgrim's serious leg injury. Thankfully, all of those injuries did not prevent any of us from completing our hike.

A few weeks after I arrived home, Pete Ross, a friend and former colleague asked, "How are you readjusting to being home?" I responded, "Well, I still sleep in my tent in the back yard, eat cold meals on the patio, and come into the house every two weeks to take a shower." He replied, "Since when does a guy have to take a shower as often as once every two weeks?" Pete may have made a valid point there. In reality, it didn't take long for me to readjust to the pleasures of life, such as air conditioning, sleeping in my own bed, and eating home-cooked meals.

I owe a debt of gratitude to all my charitable sponsors. Alzheimer's Association wrote a very nice article in their fall 2011 newsletter about my successful fund-raising of nearly $3,000 on its behalf. The Leukemia and Lymphoma Society and the Society for Melanoma Research were quite pleased with the large sums of money I raised for them too.

After returning home, Newschannel 5 in Cleveland did a lengthy television report about my hike on the evening news on September 29, 2011. The local weekly paper, The News Sun, ran a front page story on October 20, 2011, entitled, "Berea Hiker Completes the Entire Appalachian Trail with an Injury for the Last 380 Miles." If you visit http://grauathiker.blogspot.com, you may still view my television appearance, read the newspaper article, read my AT blog, see some pictures I took on the trail, and check for updates. If you are interested in purchasing a copy of this book, please visit www.grauathiker.com.

When I finished the hike, I felt that I was done hiking the trail. At this point, I can't see myself spending roughly six months again on any hike. However,

I am thinking seriously of hiking a section of the trail again, perhaps next year. After numerous and repeated requests to tell my full AT story, I decided to write this book. I can envision a hundred years from now when someone reading it says, "Wow! Buckeye Flash hiked the Appalachian Trail way back in 2011. People put gasoline into their cars in those olden days. They didn't have jet packs then, like we do today." I imagine it will be similar to what we think of now as the horse-and-buggy era of a century ago.

I have pledged proceeds from the sale of this book to Journey of Hope (JOH) in Cleveland. It is an organization that offers financial assistance to adult cancer patients to meet basic survival needs while they are undergoing cancer treatments. JOH was founded in 1999, received non-profit status in 2001, and began funding patients in 2002. The funding continues today to help fill a real need. For further information about JOH, please visit www.johcleveland.org.